A SECOND HELPING

More from Ladies, a Plate

ALEXA JOHNSTON

PENGUIN BOOKS

For Aphra Paine,
beloved niece and baking companion,
and
for the new generation
of enthusiastic home bakers

A Grace from Iona

For food that gives us life
and friends that give us love
of life,
thanks be to God.

Joy Mead, 2003

Table of Contents

Comfortable Kitchens and Happy Memories

In her 1951 book *French Country Cooking*, the incomparable Elizabeth David included a chapter on kitchen equipment – 'Batterie de Cuisine' – in which she writes: 'Some sensible person once remarked that you spend the whole of your life either in your bed or your shoes. Having done the best you can by shoes and bed, devote all the time and resources at your disposal to the building up of a fine kitchen. It will be, as it should be, the most comforting and comfortable room in the house.'*

And writing in 1974, Jane Grigson recalled: 'Before the last war, when tea was an occasion for enjoyment and not for guilt, we often used to have home-made raspberry jam sandwiches at my grandmother's house. There were always too many – raspberry jam being her favourite – and next day they would appear as pudding, having been fried in butter. I always thought, still do think, that their latter end was more glorious than their début.'**

Many readers of *Ladies, a Plate* have told me about their lasting and pleasurable memories of food and baking. These memories seem often, like Jane Grigson's, to involve grandmothers, simple food, and warm family kitchens which, in recollection at least, meet Elizabeth David's comfort requirements. And so my aim in writing this book was to continue some of the themes of *Ladies, a Plate*: that time spent in your kitchen can be a joy rather than a penance; that baking for and with others can be highly satisfying and will build lifelong memories for the recipients of your offerings; and that sharing food with family, friends, colleagues and neighbours helps build stronger communities and can contribute a little to the mental health of our society.

I believe we need to stop thinking or saying 'I've been good today' when what we mean is not that we've visited a lonely elderly friend, or given some time to a community project, but that we have resisted eating a piece of (probably commercially made) chocolate cake. My advice is this: make the chocolate cake yourself, take some to a friend and enjoy eating it together – and perhaps even go for a walk afterwards...

A Second Helping is, as the title suggests, a further selection of old-fashioned recipes written with clear instructions for a novice home baker, although experienced bakers have also told me they enjoy the step-by-step approach – and the 'Getting Ready' section of the recipes has met with widespread approval. The only addition is a 'Sweets' chapter, included because community cookbooks always seem to have a few recipes for home-made confectionery. Russian Fudge, Coconut Ice and Hokey Pokey have an enduring appeal, right up there with the commercial lollies like Spearmint Leaves, Aniseed Balls, Fizzy Fruits and Raspberries and Strawberries. (Those commercial ones are, however, definitely best left to the professionals.)

As with *Ladies, a Plate*, the sources of the recipes are primarily New Zealand home cooks who have contributed them to community cookbooks, or whose handwritten recipes have been lent to me. Some others are from my own family and friends, and a few I found in recipe books from other countries. What they have in common is that I know they all work in a home kitchen, since I have tested them at home myself – often with the delightful company of my niece, Aphra Paine. I welcomed Aphra's comments on recipe selection as well as those of my husband, Malcolm Cheadle, and my other recipe-tasting friends – and I'm very pleased with the results.

So I hope this new collection of old recipes will bring enjoyment to you – and to your family and friends. And remember that *A Second Helping* is a do-it-yourself book: I suggest you flip through it now, find a recipe you like the look of, stride purposefully into your comfortable kitchen and start baking! (Just take a moment, though, to read the next section…)

* **Elizabeth David, *French Country Cooking*, Penguin Handbooks, 1959, page 23**

** ***Jane Grigson's English Food*, Revised Edition, Penguin Books, 1993, page 279**

These Things Are Worth Knowing

The recipes in this book are all achievable in an ordinary home kitchen with a basic range of baking equipment and the ingredients are standard domestic supplies, available everywhere. Home cooks have always known that excellent results can be achieved with a little time and care – and without fancy ingredients.

FIRST OF ALL

A few preparations that don't take long, but once they are done the process of baking can flow smoothly along and you're all set to enjoy yourself.

- Always begin by reading the recipe right through – it helps to know what lies ahead.
- Turn the oven on to preheat and prepare any baking tins.
- Measure out the quantities you need of each ingredient and have them ready on the bench along with any special utensils.

INGREDIENTS

Unless the recipe specifies differently, use the following:

- Butter – salted was the New Zealand norm, but use unsalted if you prefer
- Sugar – granulated white; in most recipes you could substitute caster sugar
- Eggs – large grade
- Flour – standard flour or high grade
- Milk – full cream

MEASUREMENTS IN THIS BOOK

The first set of measurements is from the original recipe – in ounces, cups or spoons. Cup measurements in older recipes can be for a large cup, a breakfast cup, a standard cup, a small cup or a teacup. I've taken this into account in making the recipes and providing the metric conversions. The second set of measurements is metric, in grams or level spoonfuls if they are more convenient than weighing. Whichever you choose, stick with one or the other set of measurements for each recipe.

ROOM TEMPERATURE INGREDIENTS

In the 'Getting Ready' section of many of these recipes you will read the instruction to soften the butter and bring the eggs to room temperature. This is *essential*, not optional, if you want the results of your baking to live up to your expectations. Here is how I do it.

- Butter – I measure out the butter, cut it into thin slices and put it on a plate covered with a bowl – a warmed bowl in the winter – and leave it for about 20 minutes. You definitely don't want the butter to melt, just to be really soft so it will cream easily. (I don't have a microwave oven, but I am told they soften butter very quickly; just make sure you watch it closely.)
- Eggs – I put the eggs into a bowl of hot water – from the tap, not the kettle – and leave them for 10–20 minutes.
- Milk – I also make sure that milk is at room temperature, not straight from the fridge, if it is going into a cake mixture. It blends in more easily and some say it makes the cake lighter.

CREAMING THE BUTTER AND SUGAR

Combining these two ingredients into a pale, fluffy 'cream' with the sugar almost dissolved is the first step in many recipes. It really does affect the results and is worth doing properly, so always allow at least five full minutes of beating. Caster sugar is finer and dissolves more quickly than granulated, and you can use it in most recipes. If you use an electric mixer, you will need to stop it every few minutes, lift the beaters and scrape down the sides of the bowl with a spatula. Before the advent of domestic food mixers the traditional method of creaming was to sit down with a big mixing bowl on your knee and beat the butter and sugar with your (clean) hand, since its warmth speeds the process and you can feel the sugar dissolving. It is still a very efficient technique, as you will see if you try it.

WHISKING EGGS FOR A SPONGE CAKE

The terms 'whisking' and 'beating' are often used interchangeably in recipes so it is important to understand what is happening at each stage. If you are making a sponge or a meringue your first task is to aerate the egg by whisking it so it achieves maximum bulk with lots of tiny air bubbles – usually before you start adding sugar. This can be done with a wire whisk, a hand egg beater or an electric beater, but not with a wand blender as its objective is to liquidise, not to aerate. In stand mixers use the balloon whisk attachment. Keep using the same implement as you add the sugar, beating hard so it dissolves into the fluffy mixture.

CUTTING AND FOLDING

This is how you gently incorporate the sifted dry ingredients into a cake batter. The aim is to achieve a smooth amalgamation without any vigorous beating, which would collapse the air bubbles in the mixture, expand the gluten in the flour and toughen the cake. The best tool is a large metal spoon, preferably one with a shallow bowl, which will 'cut' through the mixture without squashing it. This is how you do it: Steady the bowl with one hand. Beginning with the edge of the spoon against the far side of the bowl cut down through the mixture and pull the spoon gently through the mixture towards you, scraping against the bottom of the bowl. When the spoon touches the near side of the bowl, turn it slightly and lift it up, 'folding' the mixture up and onto itself. At the same time, give the bowl a quarter-turn towards you. Keep cutting, folding and turning until everything is well combined. The transformation in the mixture is soothingly pleasant to observe and the process doesn't take long to do – or to master.

ROLLING OUT BISCUIT DOUGH OR PASTRY

Press lightly and move the rolling pin from the centre of the dough out towards the edge. Keep rotating the dough as you work, making sure it is not sticking to the bench. If it is, ease it gently upward using a plastic scraper and flick a little more flour underneath it. Don't roll back and forth. You'll just squash the dough – the idea is to stretch it out gently. For biscuits I usually roll out half the mixture at a time, which makes it easier to manage.

LINING A CAKE TIN WITH BAKING PAPER

- Square or rectangular tins – Cut two long strips of paper, each the width of the tin, and long enough to run down the side, across the bottom and up the other side, with an overhang at each end. Lay them across each other at right angles, creasing them into the lower edges of the tin.
- Circular tins – Cut two circles of paper the size of the tin's base. Cut a folded double strip of paper long enough to fit right around the inside and 2½ in/ 6 cm deeper than the tin. Make a second fold along the length of the paper, 1¼ in/3 cm from the folded edge, and use scissors to cut up to the fold at ¾ in/2 cm intervals. Fit this piece around the inside of the tin, with the cut tabs at the base. Drop the circles into the base.

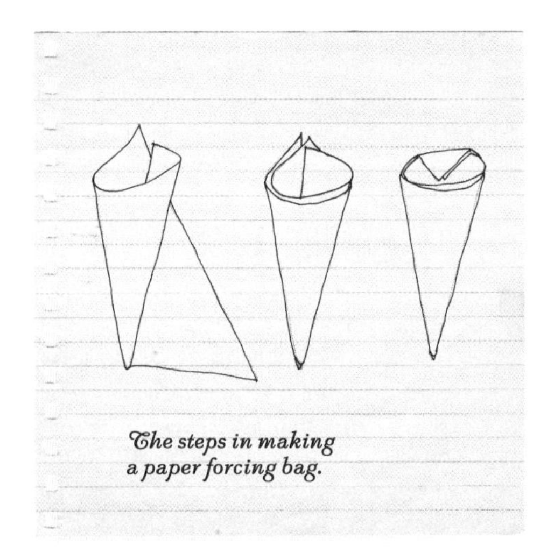

The steps in making a paper forcing bag.

MAKING A PAPER FORCING BAG

The best paper for this is luncheon wrap – not waxed or baking paper. Cut a square across the width of the paper and fold it diagonally. Roll the paper into a cone, with the point of the cone at the centre of the longest side, and secure the top edge points by folding them over. Spoon in the icing – not too much, have the bag about half-full – fold down the top to close it and force the icing down to the tip, cut off the end of the tip with a pair of scissors and squeeze away. Practice makes perfect, but I suggest holding the bag in one hand and squeezing with your thumb on top, using the index finger of the other hand to guide the point.

TO FAN OR NOT TO FAN

The fan in your oven is intended to distribute the heat more evenly and this is useful if you are baking two trays of biscuits together – the only time that I use the fan. But the fan also raises the effective temperature of the oven and has a drying effect on the baking. Be aware of this if you use the fan and compensate by reducing the temperature by about 20°F/10°C.

MELTING CHOCOLATE

The main point is not to overheat the chocolate. I chop the chocolate and put it into a heatproof bowl, then set this over a saucepan of hot water. The water should be brought to a simmer, then switched off before putting the chocolate over it. Make sure no steam can escape and condense back into the chocolate or it will 'seize' and become hard. (Again, a microwave oven may be your preference.)

FREEZING THINGS

Large cakes can usually be frozen if they are well wrapped in aluminium foil; small cakes can be frozen in containers and biscuits certainly can – either raw or cooked. Having said that, I don't freeze very much apart from biscuits and I certainly don't recommend freezing the Picnic Berry Cake since its charm lies in its warm freshness. You will need to experiment with the recipes to see which ones freeze best.

ROTATING TRAYS FOR EVEN BAKING

Even on fan-bake the heat in most ovens is slightly uneven, so trays and tins should be rotated once the mixture has risen and 'set', about halfway through the baking time. Set a timer to remind yourself to do this, and don't forget to reset it for the remaining time.

The placement of the racks inside your oven is also important. For biscuits and small cakes have the oven racks as near the centre as possible and for larger cakes, which take an hour or more to cook, have the racks below the centre. If a cake seems to be browning too quickly, before the centre is cooked, place a sheet of aluminium foil loosely on top of it to deflect the heat.

WRITING THINGS DOWN

Write your own notes in this recipe book. I know that when we were children writing in books was frowned upon, but do record your experience of a recipe: which tin worked best; how long it actually took in your oven; whether or not you used fan-bake; or who you made a cake for and when. All these will add immeasurably to the usefulness and interest of the book for you, and for your children and grandchildren should they want to use it. And if a recipe does not work for you – although I hate to imagine that this could happen – just cross it out. It's your recipe book after all.

Biscuits

Biscuits are among the simplest and easiest kinds of home baking – as well as lasting longest in the tins – and the recipes in this selection are particularly straightforward. I gathered from the responses of readers that Hokey Pokey Biscuits and Peanut Brownies were noted as omissions from *Ladies, a Plate* so here they are – both of them crisp, light and good keepers.

I've added Grantham Gingerbreads at the particular request of Joan Anderson, who embroidered the beautiful cloth that appears on the cover of this book. The recipe her mother, Marian Benton, used dates back to the 'white gingerbreads' of eighteenth century Lincolnshire and I agree with Joan that they are extremely good.

Tender and nutty Mexican Wedding Cakes arrived in New Zealand more recently, but are traditional in many European countries and deserve to be in every home baker's repertoire. So make a batch of biscuits when you get a chance and don't forget the morning mantra: 'A cup of tea without a biscuit is a missed opportunity.'

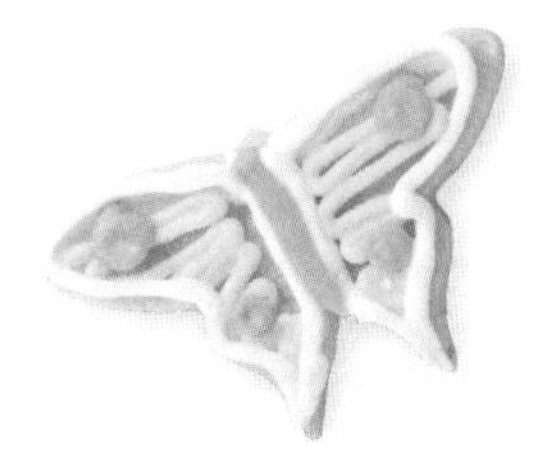

Cherry Gingers

FOR THE BISCUITS

4 oz	**butter**	**115 g**
4 oz	**soft brown sugar**	**115 g**
1	**egg**	**1**
6 oz	**flour***	**175 g**
1¼ tsp	**baking powder**	**1¼ tsp**
1 tsp	**ground ginger**	**1 tsp**
3 oz	**glacé cherries****	**85 g**
3 oz	**crystallised ginger**	**85 g**

* or use self-raising and leave out the baking powder

** For optional toppings have extra cherries and ginger cut in half, and a few squares of chocolate

When we were in our teens, my sisters and I were grateful for the pocket money we earned by babysitting for the children of our neighbours Jeanette and Colin Nicholson. Jeanette was impressively tall, elegant and beautiful, as well as being an excellent cook, and her babysitters were fortified by samples of her delicious home baking. Quite a number of my recipe index cards have Jeanette's name written on them as the recipe source and this one has remained a particular favourite. The chewy nuggets of ginger and cherries make a lovely contrast with the crisp, light biscuits and the optional garnish of a lump of chocolate, ginger or a cherry on top gives them a touch of homely glamour.

GETTING READY

Preheat the oven to 375°F/190°C and line two baking trays with baking paper or grease them lightly. Bring the butter and egg to room temperature and sift together the flour, baking powder and ground ginger. Cut the cherries into quarters and chop the crystallised ginger into pieces about the same size.

MIXING AND BAKING

1. Cream the butter and sugar until soft and light. Beat in the egg and mix well.
2. Add the sifted dry ingredients and, once they are incorporated, mix in the chopped cherries and ginger.
3. Drop heaped teaspoonfuls of the mixture onto the prepared trays, leaving a little room for spreading. If you wish, position a piece of cherry, ginger or chocolate on top of each biscuit, remembering that they may not stay centred once the biscuits are cooked – but that just adds to their charm.
4. Bake for 12–15 minutes, rotating the tray after 8 minutes. Cool on a rack and store airtight. Makes about 30.

REFRIGERATOR BISCUITS

Cherry Gingers are crisp when first baked, but they soften a little after a day or so, especially in humid Auckland where I live. If you want to make a batch that will stay crisp for longer, increase the brown sugar in the recipe to 8 oz/225 g and form the dough into a long roll in a sheet of waxed paper. Once it is inside the paper I push the sides of the dough against a ruler to make a straight-sided log which can be cut into square or rectangular biscuits. Chill the dough thoroughly, overnight if possible, then cut into thin wafers and bake at 350°F/180°C for about 8 minutes. I tend to have them as ginger biscuits when I do this, leaving out the cherries, but they could stay.

Hokey Pokey Biscuits

FOR THE BISCUITS

4 oz	butter	115 g
4 oz	sugar	115 g
1 tbsp	milk	1 tbsp
2 tsp	golden syrup	2 tsp
1 tsp	baking soda	1 tsp
½ tsp	vanilla essence	½ tsp
1 cup*	flour	170 g

* large

The revised edition of the Ideal Cookery Book was published in 1933. In her foreword Ethel Cameron wrote: 'The success and popularity of the first edition of the "Ideal Cookery Book" has proved that even in these days when Cookery Books are very numerous there is always room for a Cookery Book of special merit containing good, unusual and tested recipes, catering for all tastes.' This copy was given to me by Robyn Kelly.

Not quite as toothachingly sweet as the honeycomb toffee they are named after (see page 139 for that recipe), these crisp biscuits do have the slight fizz on the tongue created by baking soda combined with golden syrup. They are light and pleasant and undemanding and with the addition of some chopped chocolate – my sister Fiona's inspired embellishment – they are very hard to resist. I've given the traditional recipe here, but add ¾ cup of chocolate chips at the end if you wish.

GETTING READY

Preheat the oven to 350°F/180°C. Line two baking trays with baking paper or grease them lightly. Bring the butter to room temperature and sift the flour.

MIXING AND BAKING

1. Cream the butter and sugar until soft and light. Put the milk and golden syrup in a small saucepan and bring to the boil over a medium heat. Add the baking soda and stir quickly with a wooden spoon. When the mixture froths up pour it onto the butter and sugar and mix well.
2. Add the vanilla followed by the flour (and the chocolate chips if you are using them).
3. Place teaspoonfuls on the trays, allowing room for spreading, and flatten them slightly with a fork. Bake for 10–15 minutes until golden brown. Cool on a rack and store airtight. Makes about 24.

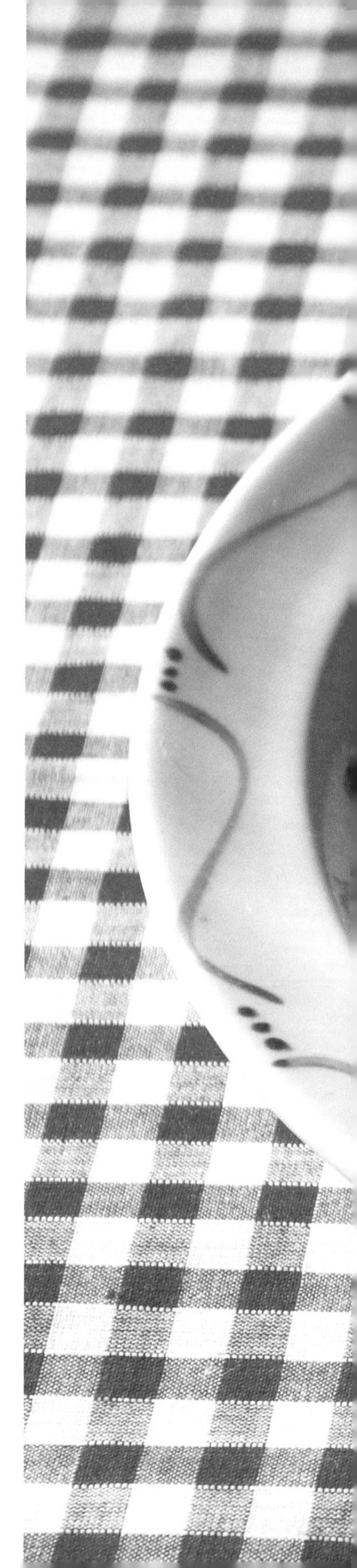

Indian Coffee Creams and Chocolate Peppermint Kisses

FOR THE BISCUITS

4 oz	butter	115 g
½ cup	sugar	100 g
1	egg	1
1 tbsp	coffee essence*	1 tbsp
2 cups	flour	250 g
1 tsp	cream of tartar	1 tsp
½ tsp	baking soda	½ tsp
2 tbsp	walnuts**	2 tbsp

* or for Chocolate Kisses replace with 1 tbsp cocoa
** or for Chocolate Kisses replace with 2 tbsp Demerara sugar

FOR THE FILLING

1 cup	icing sugar	120 g
1 tbsp	butter	15 g
1 tbsp	coffee essence†	1 tbsp

† or for Chocolate Kisses replace with 2 tsp cocoa and ¼ tsp peppermint essence

The Diner's Digest: Dishes from the World's Dinner Table, compiled by the Auckland Travel Club, New Zealand, 1941

You won't get an authentically ersatz coffee flavour in these little kisses if you use instant coffee or espresso; what's needed is coffee essence. Bushells Sweetened Coffee and Chicory Essence still comes in a tall bottle with a picture on the label of a man wearing a fez. It was widely used to make milky coffee drinks during World War II when coffee was in short supply and it contains a whopping 5 per cent coffee and 0.006 per cent chicory – the rest is caramel. Use it in the biscuits and in the filling and you'll be transported back in time – very pleasantly. Peppermint essence was also popular in New Zealand baking and I've included it in the filling for the chocolate version of these biscuits. It's the same recipe, but with different flavourings. Make them both. Mrs G. Jeavons contributed the original recipe for Indian Coffee Creams to *The Diner's Digest*, published by the Auckland Travel Club in 1941.

GETTING READY

Preheat the oven to 350°F/180°C and line two baking trays with baking paper. Measure the butter and bring it to room temperature. Sift together the flour, cream of tartar and baking soda. Chop the walnuts finely.

MIXING AND BAKING

1. Cream the butter and sugar until well combined, add the egg and coffee essence (or the cocoa mixed to a paste with 2 tbsp hot water) and beat well. Add the dry ingredients and combine to form a smooth dough. Knead the mixture until it comes together, wrap in waxed paper and put in the fridge for 10 minutes to firm up.
2. Flour the bench lightly and roll out half of the mixture – aim to have it about ¼ in/5 mm thick. Cut the dough into circles, no more than 2 in/3 cm diameter, and set them out on the baking trays. They won't spread much at all. Combine the scraps of dough and roll them out again. Repeat for the rest of the dough.
3. Sprinkle one tray of the biscuits with a few chopped walnuts and press them in very lightly with your rolling pin (or for Chocolate Kisses sprinkle with Demerara sugar). Bake for 15–20 minutes. The biscuits should be firm to the touch, slightly brown underneath and smell cooked. Cool on a rack and store airtight until you are ready to finish them.

FINISHING

1. Pair up the biscuits, matching the sizes and set them out in rows – bottoms in one row, upside down, and walnut tops next to them.
2. To make the filling, sift the icing sugar, mix in the butter and then add the coffee essence (or for Chocolate Kisses add cocoa and peppermint essence). Mix to a spreading consistency with a little hot water and beat well. Spoon about a teaspoonful of icing onto the biscuit bottoms and place the tops on, rotating them slightly to encourage the icing to spread out towards the edges. It should just be visible, not oozing everywhere. Sift a light sprinkling of icing sugar onto the Coffee Creams before serving them. Store airtight. Makes about 32 biscuits.

Melting Moments and Yo-Yos

FOR THE BISCUITS

6 oz	butter	170 g
2 oz	icing sugar	55 g
6 oz	flour	170 g
2 oz	cornflour*	55 g
1 tsp	baking powder	1 tsp

* or for Yo-Yos replace cornflour with 2 oz/55 g custard powder

FOR THE FILLING

1 tbsp**	butter	30 g
2 tbsp†	icing sugar	80 g
2 tsp	boiling water	2 tsp

** large
† heaped

AND FOR YO-YOS

2 tsp	custard powder	2 tsp

FILLING FOR YO YO'S

In a recent issue I noticed a recipe for Yo Yo's, and as I already have the recipe I thought it a good idea to pass on the filling for them. Melt one tablespoon butter and add to this a teaspoon boiling water, two large tablespoons icing sugar and one teaspoon custard powder.

Lucy Parke's recipe book contains a wealth of excellent baking advice and many delicious and reliable recipes. (Her outstanding Health Biscuits are included in Ladies, a Plate.) The method given here reduces the taste of uncooked custard powder in the Yo-Yo filling by using melted butter and boiling water. Christine Hellyar kindly lent me Lucy's book.

Melting Moments are small buttery biscuits flattened with a fork and sandwiched in pairs with jam or icing. They melt in the mouth very pleasurably and are made to the 6-2-6-2 formula, which means 6 oz butter, 2 oz icing sugar, 6 oz flour and 2 oz cornflour. To make Yo-Yos, simply substitute custard powder for the cornflour. These seem to have been called Custard Powder Biscuits until 1941, when Mrs H.N. Hewson contributed a recipe for Yo-Yos to *The Diner's Digest*. Perhaps the school playground craze for Yo-Yo toys led to a renaming. Custard powder is just cornflour that's sweetened, vanilla-flavoured and yellow-coloured, but it has a great following and is often used in New Zealand baking – as well as for making custard, of course. This recipe comes from a 1946 cookbook, *450 Favourite Recipes*, published by St Paul's Presbyterian Church in Pahiatua and sold for half a crown – or two and sixpence (25 cents). Mrs Merrie contributed the Custard Powder Biscuit recipe and she includes a little baking powder, which makes them lighter and, I think, even more palatable. The filling is from a newspaper clipping in Lucy Parke's recipe book.

GETTING READY

Preheat the oven to 350°F/180°C and line two baking trays with baking paper. Bring the butter to room temperature and sift together the icing sugar, flour, cornflour or custard powder and baking powder.

MIXING AND BAKING

1. Cream the butter until it is light and fluffy, then mix in all the dry ingredients to make a firm dough. Take teaspoonfuls of the dough and set them out on the bench. Once it is all divided up, roll each spoonful into a ball and place them in rows on the baking sheets. Flatten them well with a fork dipped in water.
2. Bake for 15–20 minutes, rotating after 10 minutes. You could also swap the trays top to bottom. After about 15 minutes the biscuits will have spread a little and should still be a very pale gold, but slightly browned on the bottom. Cool on a rack.

FINISHING

1. Pair up the biscuits, matching the sizes, and set them out in rows.
2. To make the filling, melt the butter in a small saucepan and add the boiling water. Pour this into the sifted dry ingredients and mix to form a smooth paste. Put about a teaspoonful on half of the biscuits. (Don't put the tops on until you have used up all the filling so you can distribute it evenly.) Now put the tops on, rotating them slightly to encourage the filling to spread out towards the edges. It should just be visible. Leave until the filling sets before storing in an airtight container. Makes about 36.

Grantham Gingerbreads

INGREDIENTS

4 oz	**butter**	**115 g**
8 oz	**caster sugar**	**225 g**
1	**egg***	**1**
8 oz	**flour**	**225 g**
½ oz	**ground ginger**	**4 tsp**
½ tsp	**baking soda**	**½ tsp**
pinch	**salt**	**pinch**

* **You will probably use only half of the egg.**

Grantham in Lincolnshire is famous for these biscuits. Marian Benton grew up in the nearby village of Bingham in Nottinghamshire so, when as a young woman she married and came to New Zealand, she brought the recipe with her as a reminder of home. Her daughter Joan Anderson regards them as her mother's signature recipe – although Marian's Afghans were a favourite, too, and they opened the 'Biscuits' chapter of *Ladies, a Plate*. A small biscuit is not what most people think of as a gingerbread and in New Zealand cookery books these are sometimes called Grantham Macaroons. They bear little resemblance to a chewy almond macaroon since they are very crisp – their identifying feature being that when you bite into them they have hollow centres.

Grantham Gingerbreads
½ lb flour.
½ lb castor sugar.
¼ lb butter.
½ oz ginger - 2 teaspoons
½ tesp baking soda.
1 small egg.
pinch salt.
Cream butter and sugar.
add beaten egg. Sift in
flour ginger + baking soda.
Roll into small balls.
Flatten with a fork
Bake at 300° for half an
hour - hollow centres!

This is Marian Benton's handwritten recipe and the cloth in the photograph, which also appears on the cover of this book, was made by her daughter, Joan Anderson.

GETTING READY

Preheat the oven to 300°F/150°C. Line two trays with baking paper or grease them lightly. Bring the butter and the egg to room temperature and sift together the flour, ginger and baking soda. Beat the egg with a fork in a measuring cup so it is liquid enough for you to pour half of it into the mixture.

MIXING AND BAKING

1. Cream the butter and sugar until soft and light. Mix in half the beaten egg and then the dry ingredients. The mixture should be a firm dough, but if it is too crumbly to come together, add a little more of the egg to bind it.
2. Tip the dough out of the bowl and knead lightly, then set teaspoonfuls out on the bench. Roll each spoonful into a ball and place in rows on the baking trays. Flatten slightly with a fork.
3. Bake for 30 minutes. Marian instructs that the oven should not be opened for at least 20 minutes, when you should rotate the trays and exchange them top to bottom. After 30 minutes the biscuits will be round and puffed up with pretty cracks on top, but they stay very pale. Cool on a rack and store airtight. They keep very well indeed. Makes about 50.

Mexican Wedding Cakes

INGREDIENTS

8 oz	**butter**	**225 g**
½ cup	**icing sugar**	**60 g**
½ tsp	**vanilla essence**	**½ tsp**
1⅘ cups	**flour**	**225 g**
½ tsp	**salt**	**½ tsp**
½ cup	**walnuts**	**50 g**
2 cups*	**icing sugar, extra**	**250 g**

* approximately

These little sugar-coated balls of tender walnut shortbread are nothing like our New Zealand wedding cake, but they look so pretty they could be served at almost any festive occasion. Versions of them are found in Russia, Portugal, Italy and Spain, and they began appearing in New Zealand around the mid-1970s when my cousin Marion Kitchingman found this recipe in a 1976 *New Zealand Woman's Weekly*. She made them when I was visiting Dunedin recently and I was immediately hooked. They make a very fetching gift; in an icy crystal bowl they look like a pile of snowballs; and, having tasted one, few people can resist a second – or a third. It's a good idea to make them fairly small as the icing sugar coating can deter people who are wearing dark clothing… a small biscuit is a single mouthful and less threatening. You could also make them with pecans or toasted hazelnuts – all are delicious.

GETTING READY

Preheat the oven to 400°F/200°C and line two baking trays with baking paper, or grease them lightly. Bring the butter to room temperature. Chop the nuts finely with a knife – you can do this in the food processor, but they quickly get too small and too soft, with the corners knocked off the little pieces of nut. Using a knife gives you better control and ensures the walnuts are a discernible presence in the biscuits. Sift the icing sugar.

MIXING AND BAKING

1. Cream the butter, icing sugar and vanilla until very light and fluffy. Sift in the flour and salt and mix until well combined, then mix in the nuts.
2. Use a teaspoon to make small, equally sized mounds of dough on your bench. Roll them into little balls and place in rows on the prepared baking sheets – they won't spread very much.
3. Bake for 10–12 minutes until they are firm to the touch, but not browned. Rotate the trays after 5 minutes to ensure the biscuits cook evenly. They will be a very pale golden colour when cooked. While the biscuits are in the oven, sift about 2 cups of icing sugar into a shallow dish.

FINISHING

1. Toss the biscuits in the icing sugar as soon as you can handle them – they should still be quite hot. Roll them around a few at a time, then place them on a cooling rack. Not much icing sugar will stick to begin with, but persevere. Once you have gone through the whole batch, toss them all again. More icing sugar will be sticking now and they'll look more white than golden.
2. Let them cool on the rack and then toss them in the icing sugar again. They will be looking fairly snowy by now.
3. Store airtight and dust with yet more icing sugar before you serve them. Makes about 48.

Peanut Brownies

INGREDIENTS

4 oz	butter	115 g
1 cup*	brown sugar	200 g
1	egg	1
1 cup	flour	125 g
1 tbsp	cocoa	1 tbsp
1 tsp	baking powder	1 tsp
1 cup	coconut	70 g
1 cup	raw peanuts**	150 g

* large
** with their brown skins

Mincing the roasted peanuts.

These won't be the first to disappear if you take a plate of them somewhere since they look rather dull, but keep them in an airtight tin or jar and you'll find them extremely welcome with a cup of tea. They are light and crisp, they smell good and Mrs J. Bond's recipe (from the 1941 *Diner's Digest*) with coconut and minced roasted peanuts suits me. Leave a few of the peanuts whole if you must, but this is not a chocolate peanut slab, it's a biscuit, and I think the peanuts should be part of the whole flavour, not big crunchy lumps. Still, each to their own…

GETTING READY

Preheat the oven to 350 °F/180 °C and line two baking trays with baking paper, or grease them lightly. Bring the butter to room temperature. Sift together the flour, cocoa and baking powder, add the coconut and combine well.

Lightly roast the peanuts by tipping them into a shallow tin and putting them in the oven for 10–12 minutes. Keep a close watch on them. When the skins start to split and they change colour slightly, pour them onto a clean tea towel on the bench. Rub them in the towel and when they cool a little use your hands to rub off the remaining skins. If you take them outside you can blow the papery skins away into the garden – a tip from Lois Daish. Mrs Bond instructs us to then put them through a mincer, using the coarse cutter. If a mincer isn't available, just whiz them quickly in a food processor until they are lumpy and granular.

MIXING AND BAKING

1. Cream the butter and brown sugar until really pale and fluffy, then add the egg and beat again. Add the dry ingredients a spoonful at a time and mix to a firm dough. Lastly add the roasted ground peanuts and combine well.
2. Put heaped teaspoonfuls of the mixture onto the trays, leaving some room for spreading, and flatten slightly with a fork dipped in water. Bake for 15–20 minutes. Rotate the trays after 10 minutes and swap them top to bottom. When ready, the biscuits should be firm to the touch and smell cooked. Cool on a rack and store airtight. Makes about 40 small biscuits.

Squares and Slices

Almost all the recipes in this chapter are old favourites – or variations on them. Tan Squares, Marshmallow Slices and Dream Kisses have been made in New Zealand kitchens for almost a century and Chinese Chew is another baking tin staple. Anzac Bars and Princess Fingers are inspired versions of Anzac Biscuits and Louise Cake and, although originally from America, Lemon Bars are included in most community recipe books and feel like a local invention.

Chocolate Brownies, however, remain an American speciality and I was fortunate in having an American/New Zealand friend, Laura Kroetsch, contribute to this chapter her perfected recipe for a really rich and fudgy version. You won't be disappointed by any of these easily made and delicious treats.

NANAIMO NOTE

In the 'Fingers, Squares and Slices' chapter of *Ladies, a Plate*, I included a recipe for Nainoma Bars that a friend had given me, but which also appears in dozens of community recipe books around New Zealand. I didn't know the source of the recipe, but a number of readers kindly let me know that the original version of this layered slice – a crushed-biscuit fudge base with custard-powder-flavoured icing topped with melted chocolate – was the Nanaimo Bar, named after the city of that name on Vancouver Island. I am happy to concede that New Zealand (and Australia) took over a good recipe and managed to mangle its name, but I did discover one significant difference between the Canadian and Antipodean versions. In Canada the base is made with Graham Cracker crumbs, whereas here the recipes stipulate crushed malt biscuits. Graham Crackers were always a mystery ingredient to me when I looked at American recipes, but I now know they are close to what we would call a wholemeal digestive biscuit – very different from our malt biscuits. So perhaps we could venture that New Zealand's Nainoma Bars have some slight claim to a different name…

Anzac Bars or Autumn Fingers

INGREDIENTS

½ cup*	**flour**	**70 g**
½ cup*	**coconut**	**45 g**
1 cup*	**rolled oats**	**100 g**
2 oz	**walnuts**	**60 g**
pinch	**salt**	**pinch**
½ cup	**brown sugar**	**100 g**
¼ cup	**sugar**	**50 g**
4 oz	**butter**	**115 g**
2 tsp	**golden syrup**	**30 g**
½ tsp	**baking soda**	**½ tsp**
½ tsp	**vanilla essence**	**½ tsp**

* **breakfast cup**

Often called Oat Fingers or Oatina Crisp, these are the bar version of the Anzac Biscuit and are made with many variations. Elizabeth Messenger named them Autumn Fingers in her *Evening Post* recipe column 'Dine With Elizabeth'. She published the recipe in April 1957 and no doubt the name seemed appropriate since their colour is indeed autumnal and they have a delightfully crisp, dry texture. She says she wrote one word on her recipe testing notes: 'Gorgeous!' I've halved the quantities in Elizabeth's version to make just one tin, but you'll still have plenty to share. They stay fresh and crunchy for up to a month in an airtight tin or jar.

GETTING READY

Preheat the oven to 350°F/180°C and line a shallow 12 x 8 in/30 x 21 cm tin with baking paper, or grease it lightly. Chop the walnuts.

MIXING AND BAKING

1. Combine the flour, coconut, rolled oats, walnuts and salt in a large bowl. Add the sugars and mix well.
2. Put the butter, golden syrup and sifted baking soda in a saucepan and melt gently together over a medium heat, stirring with a wooden spoon, until the mixture begins to froth. Pour it onto the dry ingredients and add the vanilla essence.
3. Stir until everything is combined and press the mixture evenly into the prepared tin and bake for 15–20 minutes until it is golden brown, rotating the tin after 10 minutes. Try not to overcook it.
4. Cut into bars while hot, pressing the edges gently back down if they roughen. Cool in the tin and store airtight. Makes 24.

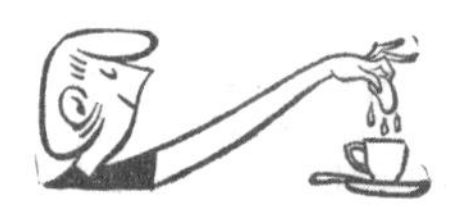

APRIL

Crisp and delightful

IF you like nutty brown bread made with coarse meal, you'll just love this companion piece in biscuits, autumn fingers. I find that across my testing notes for these I have written "gorgeous"; not perhaps a very literary description of a biscuit, but sufficiently expressive! The recipe makes a large batch of bars which are a little bit crisp and a little bit "chewy" and altogether delightful.

AUTUMN FINGERS

8oz. butter
1 rounded tablespoon golden syrup
1 teaspoon soda
1 breakfast cup flour
1 breakfast cup coconut
2 breakfast cups coarse oatmeal
4oz. walnuts
½ teaspoon salt
½ teaspoon maple essence (or vanilla)
1 cup (packed) brown sugar
½ cup white sugar

KOWHAI

Laura's Chocolate Brownies

INGREDIENTS

8 oz	dark chocolate*	225 g
3 oz	unsalted butter	85 g
6½ oz	sugar	180 g
pinch**	salt	⅛ tsp
2	eggs	2
1 tsp	vanilla essence	1 tsp
2 oz	flour	55 g
2–4 oz	walnuts†	55–115 g
2 oz	dark chocolate, extra	55 g

* Laura suggests using a good quality chocolate with at least 70% cocoa butter.
** a good pinch
† chopped into largish pieces

I wanted to include a Chocolate Brownie recipe in this chapter and so called on an American friend, Laura Kroetsch, originally from North Carolina and now a Wellington resident, for her best one. A brilliant home baker, she kindly gave me this recipe in which she toasts the walnuts slightly and uses a lot of very dark chocolate, making the finished square less sweet and more intensely chocolate. It cuts neatly into bars, keeps well and has the requisite slightly crisp finish on the top. This is the Chocolate Brownie for me.

GETTING READY

Preheat the oven to 335°F/170°C. Place the walnuts on a baking tray and toast them in the heating oven for about 6 minutes. Grease a shallow 8 x 8 in/20 x 20 cm square cake tin and line it with a piece of baking paper, making sure there is enough paper above the edge of the tin to allow you to lift the Brownie out in one piece. Butter the paper. Bring the butter and eggs to room temperature, sift the flour and break the chocolate into smallish pieces.

MIXING AND BAKING

1. Put the chocolate and butter in a double boiler or a medium-sized heatproof bowl set over gently simmering water. Stir occasionally with a wooden spoon until the mixture is melted and smooth.
2. Remove from the heat and mix in the sugar and salt, beating well with the wooden spoon, then beat in the eggs one at a time.
3. Add the vanilla and flour and keep beating until the mixture becomes very shiny and leaves the sides of the bowl. This should take only a minute or so. Fold in the toasted walnuts and the extra chopped chocolate and pour into the prepared tin.
4. Bake for 30–35 minutes or until a fine skewer comes out moist but clean, with no batter sticking to it. Don't overcook! As Laura says, 'Brownies are best when moist and fudgy.'
5. Cool in the tin on a rack for about 10 minutes, then remove the whole slab from the tin and cool completely before cutting into fingers or squares. Laura suggests this makes 12 big Brownies or 16 more reasonably sized ones. I cut it into 24 bars.

AN AMERICAN CLASSIC
Chocolate Brownies, really rich fudgy ones, are an intrinsic part of American home baking. New Zealanders seem to have discovered Brownies after World War II since the Women's Institutes *Home Cookery Book* of 1945 includes 'Chocolate Cooky – American Recipe' and Aunt Daisy's 1947 *NEW Cookery* book has 'Fudge Cake (Californian)'. These both included chocolate, but many of the later versions of Brownies in New Zealand community cookbooks use cocoa rather than chocolate in the mix and have a cake-like texture – a little too dry for the Fudgy Brownie enthusiast. If you are going to make Brownies, I think you do need chocolate.

Dream Kisses and Frivolities

FOR THE BASE

½ cup	brown sugar	100 g
2 cups	flour	250 g
6 oz	butter	170 g

FOR THE TOPPING

3	eggs	3
1 cup	brown sugar	200 g
1 cup	coconut	70 g
1 cup	walnuts	100 g
1 tbsp	flour	1 tbsp
1 tsp	baking powder	1 tsp

The kisses in New Zealand recipe books are usually biscuits and small cakes sandwiched together in pairs, but these are kisses of a different kind – they have two complementary layers baked together. Dream Kisses have a shortcake base under a topping of eggs, brown sugar, coconut, walnuts and sometimes dried fruit as well. I have found them, with slight variations in the quantities of sugar and the presence or absence of baking powder in the base, in several of Aunt Daisy's books from the 1930s; in *450 Favourite Recipes* from Pahiatua Presbyterian Church in 1946; in the 1965 Women's Division of Federated Farmers' 1965 cookery book; and in several manuscript recipe books. Frivolities, from Elizabeth Messenger's *Evening Post* column 'Dine With Elizabeth', 1 May 1956, are very similar but have a delicious hint of lemon in the topping. Both are extremely popular and very simple to put together.

GETTING READY

Preheat the oven to 350°F/180°C and line a shallow tin with baking paper, or grease it lightly. Chop the walnuts for the topping, keeping them fairly coarse.

MIXING AND BAKING

1. Combine the sugar and flour and rub in the butter with your fingertips – or use the food processor. Stop when it begins to form into clumps. Put the mixture into the tin and press down firmly and evenly.
2. Bake for 15–20 minutes until it is just beginning to brown at the edges. Remove from the oven and cool slightly on a rack.

TO MAKE THE TOPPING

1. Beat together the eggs and brown sugar until they are pale and fluffy – use an egg beater. Fold in the remaining ingredients and spread the mixture onto the warm base. Return it to the oven and cook for a further 20–25 minutes until the topping is golden brown. Rotate the tray after 15 minutes. Cool in the tin on a wire rack.
2. Cut into fingers when cold and store airtight. Makes about 24.

FOR FRIVOLITIES

The base is the same, but change the topping as follows: Use 2 eggs, leave out the flour and baking powder and add 1 cup/170 g chopped raisins, ¼ tsp salt, 1 tsp grated lemon zest and 2 tbsp lemon juice. Shredded coconut rather than ordinary desiccated is an improvement. (Elizabeth Messenger described them thus: 'Frivolities are their name and frivolous their nature; but they are like a gay scarlet umbrella on a wet and dreary day…')

Fly Cemeteries

FOR THE BASE AND TOP

1¾ cups	flour	200 g
2 oz	caster sugar	55 g
4½ oz	butter	125 g
1	egg yolk	1
2 tsp	cold water	2 tsp

FOR JEAN CAMPBELL'S FILLING (LOIS DAISH'S VERSION)

2 cups	mixed, dried fruit*	275g
1	smallish tart apple**	1
1 tsp	cocoa	1 tsp
½ tsp	ground cloves	½ tsp

* sultanas, raisins, currants, figs
** peeled, cored and chopped

FOR MRS CADDIE'S FILLING

2 tbsp	blackcurrant jam	2 tbsp
2 tbsp	brown sugar	2 tbsp
¾ lb	currants	340 g

The chief prerequisite for a successful Fly Cemetery is a dense and dark filling – with individual raisin 'flies' appropriately squashed together. The enclosing layers come in several forms: some recipe books suggest plain pastry – shortcrust on the bottom and flaky on the top; others a sweet short pastry or a more cakey mixture. I really like Lois Daish's version. She adapted it slightly from a recipe she found in *Mackenzie Muster: A Century of Favourites* (from the South Island's Mackenzie Country), published in 1985 to raise funds for a community centre in Fairlie, South Canterbury. The original recipe came from Jean Campbell. Jean's filling uses mixed dried fruit, apple and spice and tastes very good indeed. In an earlier South Island book, sold in 1967 to benefit the Karitane Public Hall Building Committee, I found another excellent filling contributed by Mrs Caddie. She suggests currants mixed with blackcurrant jam and a little brown sugar – very simple and effective. Try them both. You can call them Fruit Squares if you wish, but for me they'll always be Fly Cemeteries.

GETTING READY

Preheat the oven to 375°F/190°C. Make the first filling by pulsing all the ingredients in a food processor, or chop the dried fruit a little, grate the apple and mix everything together to a rough paste. If you are making Mrs Caddie's filling, just combine everything in a bowl, using enough of the jam to stick it all together.

MIXING AND BAKING

1. Put the flour and sugar into a food processor, drop in the cold butter in small lumps and pulse until the mixture is like breadcrumbs, then tip out onto the bench. Or you could rub the butter in with your fingertips. Mix the egg yolk and cold water with a fork and sprinkle over the floury mixture. Fork through, then use your hands to press the dough together and knead lightly until it is smooth.
2. Divide the mixture in two and, on separate pieces of baking paper, roll out each to a rough circle or square, about 23 cm across. Put one layer on a baking tray. Spread the filling evenly over the base, leaving a margin at the edges, then invert the top layer of pastry onto the fruit, remove the paper and press the edges together well. Prick the top layer with a fork.
3. Bake for about 25 minutes, rotating the tray after 15 minutes. Cool on a rack and slice to serve. Keeps well in an airtight tin. Makes about 16 squares or wedges.

Lemon Bars

FOR THE BASE

6 oz	**butter**	**170 g**
¾ cup	**icing sugar**	**105 g**
1½ cups	**flour**	**180 g**

FOR THE TOPPING

2 oz	**butter**	**55g**
1 cup	**caster sugar**	**200g**
1½ tbsp	**flour**	**15 g**
3	**lemons**	**3**
3	**eggs**	**3**

Very pale and pretty, yet delivering a penetrating citrusy tang, these combine the unctuous appeal of lemon honey with a crisply tender biscuit base. I've given two methods for making them. The first version is simpler to do but the second version gives a more definite textural contrast between base and topping. Both are delicious. Several of the older cookery books have little lemon tartlets – shortcrust pastry cases filled with lemon honey and then baked. A dollop of whipped cream on top was mandatory. But these slim golden bars are less trouble to make and can be served with a pristine dusting of icing sugar – or a more daring drizzle of dark chocolate.

GETTING READY

Preheat the oven to 375°F/180°C and line a shallow 12 x 8 in/30 x 21 cm tin with baking paper, or grease it lightly. Finely grate the zest of two of the lemons and squeeze the juice of all three.

MIXING AND BAKING

1. Combine the base ingredients in a food processor, or rub the butter into the dry ingredients and work into a smooth paste with your fingers. It should be fairly soft and malleable. Press the dough evenly into the prepared tin and put in the oven to bake for 15–20 minutes, until it is lightly golden. Don't overcook, as it is going back into the oven later.
2. Combine the topping ingredients in a bowl, mixing with a fork until well amalgamated. (If you prepare the topping in advance, make sure to mix it again before you pour it on or all the sugar will stay at the bottom of the bowl.)
3. Pour the mixture onto the hot biscuit base and return to the oven for another 30 minutes. Rotate the tray after 15 minutes.
4. Remove the tray from the oven and set on a wire rack to cool in the tin. Dust the top with sifted icing sugar or wait until it cools and drizzle the top with melted dark chocolate. See page 10 for instructions on melting chocolate.
5. Cut into bars. Store airtight and preferably in the fridge. Makes 24 bars.

ALTERNATIVE METHOD

1. Bake the base for 20–25 minutes until fully cooked and golden brown. Remove from the oven and reduce the oven temperature to 300°F/150°C. Rest the tin on a rack while you make the topping.
2. Put the butter, sugar, flour and lemon juice and rind in the top of a double boiler set over simmering water. Stir until the butter melts and everything is nicely combined. Remove from the heat.
3. Beat the eggs in a small bowl until they are liquid. Ladle a little of the hot mixture onto the eggs, stirring well, then pour it all back into the double boiler, and return to the heat. Stir over still-simmering water until the mixture thickens and then pour it onto the shortcake base. Return to the oven for 10–15 minutes until the topping is just set.
4. Cool in the tin, chill and then cut into bars. Makes 24.

Marshmallow Slice

FOR THE BASE

4 oz	**butter**	**115 g**
4 oz	**sugar**	**115 g**
½ tsp	**vanilla essence**	**½ tsp**
2	**egg yolks**	**2**
1½ cups	**flour***	**225 g**
1 tsp	**baking powder**	**1 tsp**
pinch	**salt**	**pinch**

* breakfast cup

FOR THE MARSHMALLOW TOPPING

1 oz	**gelatine**	**30 g**
½ pint	**cold water**	**230 ml**
4 oz	**icing sugar**	**115 g**
2	**egg whites**	**2**
pinch	**salt**	**pinch**

FLAVOURINGS

½ tsp	**peppermint essence**	**½ tsp**
2 oz	**dark chocolate**	**55 g**
	a few chopped walnuts	
OR		
	the juice of a lemon	
2 tbsp	**red jam**	**2 tbsp**
¼ cup	**coconut, slightly toasted in a dry frying pan**	**20 g**

You can make these fluffy slices in a variety of flavours on the same biscuit base. Marshmallow is not difficult to make, but you need an electric beater to whisk it – a food processor won't do. Some recipes include egg white and in others you just whip up the gelatine and sugar-syrup mixture. Both work, but the egg white makes the marshmallow slightly firmer in my view and, since I use two yolks in the biscuit base, I use the whites in the marshmallow.

GETTING READY

Preheat the oven to 350 °F/180 °C and line a shallow 12 x 8 in/ 30 x 21 cm tin with baking paper, or grease it lightly. Bring the butter to room temperature.

MIXING AND BAKING

1. Cream the butter and sugar until pale and fluffy, then beat in the vanilla essence followed by the egg yolks.
2. Sift in the flour, baking powder and salt and work everything together to form a paste.
3. Press evenly into the prepared tin and bake for about 15 minutes or until golden brown and cooked.

FINISHING

1. Put the gelatine, water and icing sugar into the top of a double boiler, or use a heatproof mixing bowl which will fit over a saucepan. Bring the water in the saucepan to a swift boil, put the bowl on top and stir until the gelatine and sugar are completely dissolved. Remove from the heat and set aside.
2. Put the egg whites into a large bowl and whisk until stiff with an electric beater, adding a pinch of salt and either the peppermint essence or the lemon juice at the end. Now pour the slightly cooled gelatine mixture onto the egg whites and whisk again until the mixture is cold, very white and very fluffy.
3. Pour it onto the shortcake base (which you have spread with a thin layer of jam if you are making the lemon version).
4. Sprinkle the marshmallow with toasted coconut and leave until set – or allow to cool before spreading with a thin layer of melted dark chocolate and dusting with finely chopped walnuts.
5. Cut into fingers using a sharp knife and wiping the blade between each cut. Store airtight. Makes about 24 bars.

Princess Fingers

FOR THE BASE

4 oz	**butter**	**115 g**
3 oz	**sugar**	**85 g**
2	**egg yolks**	**2**
8 oz	**flour**	**225 g**
½ tsp	**baking powder**	**½ tsp**

FOR THE FILLING

3-4 tbsp	**raspberry jam**	**3-4 tbsp**
½ cup	**glacé cherries**	**80 g**
½ cup	**walnuts**	**50 g**

FOR THE TOPPING

2	**egg whites**	**2**
pinch	**salt**	**pinch**
½ cup	**sugar**	**100 g**
½ cup	**coconut**	**40 g**
1 cup	**rice bubbles**	**25 g**
1	**orange**	**1**

Contributors' names do not appear in the 1939 *Home Cookery Book* compiled by the New Zealand Women's Institutes, but whoever thought up this version of Louise Cake was truly inspired. The rice bubbles disappear into the meringue, but add a pleasant crispness; the red cherries peep seductively through the white topping and the inclusion of orange zest is a master stroke. Fit for a princess indeed.

GETTING READY

Preheat the oven to 350°F/180°C and line a shallow 12 x 8 in/ 30 x 21 cm tin with baking paper, or grease it lightly. Bring the butter to room temperature. Chop the cherries and walnuts. Finely grate the zest from the orange – you need 2–3 teaspoonfuls.

MIXING AND BAKING

1. Cream the butter and sugar together until light and fluffy, then add the egg yolks and mix well. Add the sifted flour and baking powder and combine to make a smooth dough. Press the dough evenly into the tin. Spread the jam over the base – it won't be a very thick layer – and sprinkle it evenly with the cherries and walnuts.
2. Make the topping by whisking the egg whites with the salt until they are stiff, then fold in the sugar, coconut, rice bubbles and orange zest. Spoon the mixture onto the cherries and walnuts, and spread it carefully around. It won't cover them completely, but try to get a thin layer over everything.
3. Bake for about 20 minutes, rotating the tray after 10 minutes. When it is cooked, the coconut should be lightly golden.
4. Cut into fingers once it is cold. Store airtight. Makes 32 fingers.

Chinese Chew

INGREDIENTS

2	eggs	2
1 cup	brown sugar	200 g
2 tbsp	butter	30 g
pinch	salt	pinch
1 tsp	vanilla essence	1 tsp
1 cup	flour	125 g
½ tsp	baking powder	½ tsp
1 cup	dates	120 g
1 cup	walnuts	100 g
¾ cup	ginger	100 g
2 tbsp	milk	30 ml
	icing sugar, for dusting	

With or without butter, with or without ginger, with brown or white sugar – Chinese Chew seems to have been continually hybridising since it appeared in New Zealand and Australian recipe books in the early 1940s. I imagined it was called 'Chinese' because of the inclusion of preserved ginger, but several of the earlier versions have none. Dates and walnuts are the constants and it's the dates that make it chewy. The following recipe is a further hybrid, my version of the one in *Aunt Daisy's Radio Cookery Book*, 9th edition, circa 1939, with a small amount of melted butter for tenderness and lots of ginger for bite.

GETTING READY

Preheat the oven to 400°F/200°C and line a shallow 12 x 8 in/30 x 21 cm tin with baking paper, or grease it lightly. Bring the eggs to room temperature. Sift the flour and baking powder. Chop the walnuts, ginger and dates. Melt the butter.

MIXING AND BAKING

1. Whisk the eggs and sugar together, using an electric or a hand beater, until they are well combined and slightly fluffy (about 2 minutes). Change to a large metal spoon and fold in the melted butter, salt and vanilla essence followed by the sifted flour and baking powder, and lastly the fruit, nuts, ginger and the milk.
2. Spread in the prepared tin and bake for 15–20 minutes. Rotate the tin after 10 minutes. When the cake is lightly browned and springy to the touch, remove it from the oven and leave to cool on a wire rack.
3. Cut into bars while it is still just warm, pressing the edges back into position if they roughen when cutting. Sprinkle with icing sugar to serve. Store airtight. Makes about 24 bars.

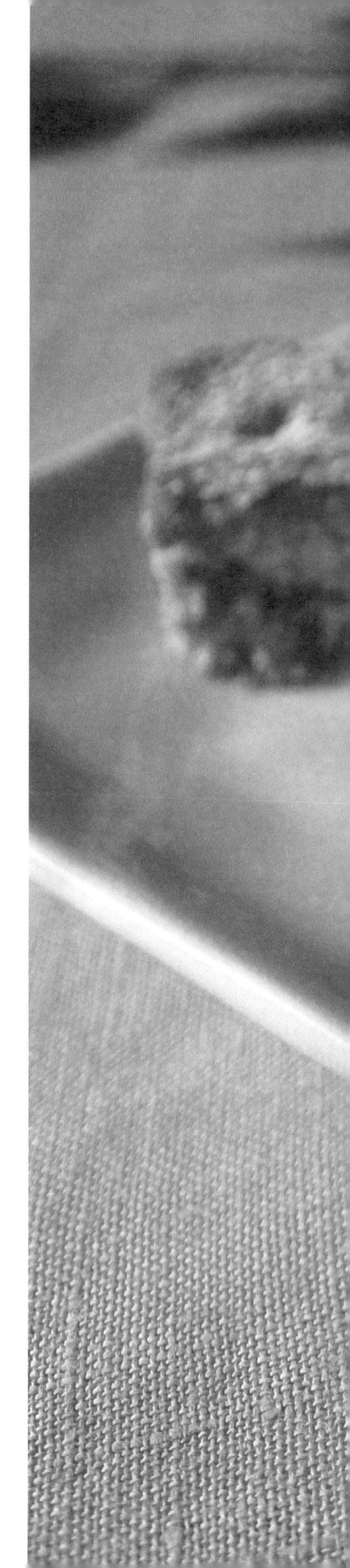

Tan Squares

FOR THE BASE AND TOPPING

6 oz	butter	170 g
3 oz	sugar	85 g
½ tsp	vanilla essence	½ tsp
10 oz	flour	280 g
2 tbsp	walnuts	10 g
6 squares	dark chocolate	30 g

FOR THE FILLING

2 oz	butter	55 g
1 tbsp	golden syrup	1 tbsp
½ tin	sweetened condensed milk	200 g

This chapter ends with a classic layered slice found in many community recipe books. Some of the shortcake base mixture is kept back and sprinkled on top of the caramel filling, with the addition of chopped chocolate and walnuts. You could transform the mixture by substituting 3 tbsp cocoa for 3 tbsp of the flour, or use jam or lemon honey in place of the caramel filling. All are worth making.

GETTING READY

Preheat the oven to 350°F/180°C and line a shallow tin with baking paper, or grease it lightly. Bring the butter to room temperature. Chop the walnuts and chocolate.

MIXING AND BAKING

1. Cream the butter and sugar until soft and fluffy, add the vanilla essence and work in the flour to form a soft paste.
2. Weigh the mixture, remove one-third to use for the topping and set it aside in a covered bowl in the fridge to chill slightly.
3. Press the remaining mix into the prepared tin and chill while you make the filling.
4. Put the filling ingredients in a saucepan and stir over a gentle heat until they have melted together. Set aside to cool to room temperature and then spread over the chilled base.
5. Crumble the reserved topping mixture into a bowl, mix with the walnuts and chocolate, and sprinkle evenly over the caramel. If the mixture is too firm to crumble easily, then grate it coarsely. Bake for 35 minutes, rotating after 20 minutes, until the topping is an appropriately tan colour. Cut into squares or fingers while warm and leave in the tin until cold. Store airtight. Makes 16 large squares or 32 fingers.

Small Cakes

In this mix of memorable old favourites and a few less familiar treats, I have updated some but left the real classics alone – they need no tampering with. After more than a century of adorning tea tables, Sponge Kisses and Cream Lilies are still quick and inexpensive to make and invariably greeted with delight when they appear today. Chocolate Crackles were a staple at every birthday party in my childhood, but the recipe I've given here, using dark chocolate and a little peppermint essence is, I think, an improvement on the 1950s version.

Harmony Tarts and Matrimony Tarts live up to their delicious names and Portuguese Custard Tarts, while not a New Zealand tradition, are so well loved that we should all know how to make them. The combination of a very light and flaky cream cheese pastry with Lois Daish's smooth golden custard filling ensures total perfection.

When I began baking in earnest in the 1960s I was tormented by a tantalising recipe for Maple Walnut Cup Cakes since imitation maple syrup was all we could get in New Zealand. Now that the real thing is available everywhere, these little cakes have come into their own and are a decorative and delectable small indulgence. And lastly a trio of recipes that turn a leftover egg white or two into batches of chewy or crunchy morsels. Versions of these appear in most community cookbooks and are proof that the creativity of home cooks with limited resources knows no bounds. As home bakers today we have a lot to live up to – so start with a few of these recipes and you will be on the path to afternoon-tea perfection.

Apricot Crescents

FOR THE CREAM CHEESE PASTRY

4 oz	**butter**	**115 g**
3 oz	**cream cheese**	**85 g**
1 cup	**flour**	**125 g**

FOR THE FILLING AND TO FINISH

2–3 tbsp	**apricot jam**	**2–3 tbsp**
1	**egg**	**1**
2 tbsp	**walnuts**	**2 tbsp**
	icing sugar, for dusting	

I found this recipe lurking at the bottom of a page in the 1964 *Menorah Cookbook*, a compendium of excellent recipes published to help raise funds for a new synagogue in Auckland. It is in the 'Coffee Accompaniments' chapter, modestly called Cream Cheese Envelope and contributed by Mrs H. Rosen. Mrs Rosen's pastry was a revelation to me – tender, light, flakily layered and with a slight cream cheese tang, it is made in a moment in a food processor or mixer and, having rested overnight in the fridge, it can be rolled out with ease. I suggest you try your home-made Apricot Jam in these (recipe on page 122), although any good, tart jam will do and Guava Jelly is excellent.

MAKING THE PASTRY THE DAY BEFORE YOU NEED IT

Bring the butter and cream cheese to room temperature – they don't have to be very soft, just not completely chilled – then cream them together in a food processor or by hand. Add the flour and pulse or mix to combine. Turn out onto the bench, knead lightly, divide in half and form into two flat, round discs about ½ in/1 cm thick. Wrap well in waxed paper and refrigerate overnight or for at least 2 hours.

GETTING READY

Remove the pastry from the fridge and leave on the bench in its paper for 20 minutes before rolling it out. Preheat the oven to 375°F/190°C. Line two baking trays with baking paper or grease them lightly. Stir up the apricot jam to loosen it and beat the egg for the glaze. Use a food processor to grind the walnuts into crumbs or chop finely.

MAKING AND BAKING THE CRESCENTS

1. Take one disc of pastry and roll it gently on a floured board into a circle about ⅛ in/3 mm thick and 8–9 in/20–23 cm in diameter. Try to keep it as round as you can – you could use the flat base of a flan tin as a circular pattern.
2. Spread half the apricot jam evenly over the round of dough and then, using a long-bladed knife, cut the pastry into 8 or 12 wedges, just as you would cut up a pie.
3. Take each wedge and, starting at the wide end, roll it up fairly tightly towards the point. Finish with the point underneath, bend the roll into a shallow crescent and place on the tray.
4. You can make up the second lot of pastry the same way, or cut it into squares or rounds, place a small half-teaspoonful of jam on one half and fold over to enclose the jam. Pinch the edges to seal and place on the baking tray. Chill the pastries on the trays for 20 minutes.
5. Remove the trays from the fridge, brush each pastry lightly with the egg and sprinkle with the walnuts. Bake for 10–12 minutes until golden brown, rotating the trays halfway through.
6. Cool on a rack and dust with icing sugar before serving. They are wonderful warm and at their best on the day they are made. Makes 16–24 crescents.

CREAM CHEESE PASTRY

Once I began making this pastry I discovered it is a classic European recipe and that in Polish cooking cream cheese pastry crescents made with a variety of fruit fillings are called Rugelach. The earliest New Zealand version of the pastry I found was in the 'Home Interests' column of the *Otago Witness* of 5 February 1902, which had a recipe for German Puff Pastry made with sour cream rather than cream cheese. The writer of the recipe says: 'It can be used instead of ordinary puff paste for fruit pies, tarts, etc.'

Chocolate Crackles and Birdnests

FOR THE CHOCOLATE CRACKLES

1 oz	**butter**	**25 g**
3½ oz	**dark chocolate**	**100 g**
¼ tsp	**peppermint essence**	**¼ tsp**
2 cups	**rice bubbles**	**50 g**

BIRDNESTS

As a young baker I was attracted by the inventive name and the simplicity of this recipe when I found it in the 'Small Cakes' section of *Tastefully Yours*, a 1963 recipe book of my mother's from the parish of Waverley in Invercargill. Birdnests are made from baked cornflakes, which turn a very bright gold in their coating of butter, brown sugar and honey, and acquire a fantastically sharp crunch as well. The instructions in the recipe are to press them with the handle of a knife when they come out of the oven to make a nest shape and then fill them with whipped cream. I have never taken them this far but it could be worth a try.

When I was growing up a birthday party without Chocolate Crackles was not a real party. I clearly remember the sick feeling brought on by having eaten too many of them – even as I reached for another – and the impossibility of resisting one last lick of the spoon while making them. In New Zealand, icing sugar, cocoa and melted white vegetable fat were the binding ingredients for the rice bubbles, while in Australia desiccated coconut was also essential. Nowadays I prefer to use melted chocolate with a little butter added and a dash of peppermint. I make them quite small, too. This means you can eat more of them, of course, and I haven't had any complaints from children – or from adults.

MIXING

1. Put 16 regular-sized paper cases – or 32 tiny ones – into patty tins. Melt the butter and chopped chocolate in a heatproof bowl over simmering water. Stir with a wooden spoon until smooth, then add the peppermint essence.
2. Remove the bowl from the heat and mix in the rice bubbles until everything is well combined. Spoon the mixture into the paper cases, piling it fairly high. Put them in the fridge to set, but take them out for a few minutes before serving. The chocolate looks dull when you chill it, but regains its shine at room temperature. Makes 16 large or 32 small Chocolate Crackles.

FOR THE BIRDNESTS

5 oz	cornflakes	140 g
3 oz	butter	85 g
2 oz	brown sugar	55 g
1 tbsp	honey	20 g

GETTING READY

Preheat the oven to 350°F/180°C and put 18 regular-sized paper cases or 36 tiny ones into patty tins.

MIXING AND BAKING

1. Place the cornflakes in a large bowl. Melt together the butter, sugar and honey, pour them on the cornflakes and mix to combine.
2. Spoon the mixture carefully into the paper cases and bake for 10 minutes. Remove from the oven, cool on a rack and store airtight. Makes 18 large or 36 small Birdnests.

Cream Lilies

FOR THE CAKES

3	**eggs**	**3**
1 cup	**caster sugar**	**200 g**
1 cup	**flour**	**125 g**
1 tsp	**baking powder**	**1 tsp**
pinch	**salt**	**pinch**

FOR FINISHING

½ pint	**cream**	**300 ml**
2 slices	**tinned peach**	**2 slices**
OR		
½ pkt	**lemon jelly crystals**	**½ pkt**
	icing sugar, for dusting	

Cream Lilies also appear in the Bridal Edition de Luxe of Tried Recipes from the Victoria League, which includes 'extra Recipes suitable for two'. The introduction describes the Victoria League as 'named in memory of the late Queen Victoria. Its aim is to foster every movement which makes for union between the United Kingdom and her overseas Dominions.' This copy was a gift from Dorothy and Patricia to Gladys Grayson before her wedding to Ernest Thomas in April 1930 and it was given to me by Gladys's daughter Trish Gribben.

These were always a sign of an accomplished baker. Elegant, delicious and slightly whimsical, they mimic the shape of the beautiful calla or arum lilies, which unfurl each spring under trees and near damp hollows in farm paddocks all over the North Island. They are small sponge cakes rolled into cones as soon as they come out of the oven, then filled with whipped cream and adorned with a piece of yellow jelly or tinned peach for the centre of the lily. Slightly excessive, perhaps, and not for the novice, but work your way up to them. Cream Lilies seem to have fallen out of favour after the 1950s, but I found recipes for them in most of my earlier cookery books. This one is from the 1941 *Diner's Digest*, produced by the Auckland Travel Club, which was famed for the high quality of its afternoon teas. The recipe's contributor was Mrs J.H. Quinn.

GETTING READY

Preheat the oven to 400°F/200°C and line two baking trays with baking paper, or grease them lightly. Bring the eggs to room temperature. Cut the peach slices into small strips or make up the jelly with half the usual amount of water, leave it to set firmly in a shallow plate, then cut it into small strips. Sift together the flour and baking powder – twice.

MIXING AND BAKING

1. Separate the whites and yolks of the eggs. Beat the yolks and sugar with an electric beater in a warm bowl for at least 5 minutes until creamy. In another large bowl whisk the egg whites until stiff and then add the beaten yolks and sugar.
2. Keep beating until well blended, then remove the beaters. Sift the dry ingredients on and fold them through using a shallow metal spoon.
3. Drop the mixture onto the prepared trays from the tip of a dessertspoon in circles about 3 in/7 cm diameter, four to a tray and allowing room for spreading. Bake for about 8–9 minutes until risen and pale gold. They should be just beginning to brown at the edges.
4. Remove them from the trays with a thin-bladed knife or a fine spatula while they are still hot and bend each one quickly into the shape of a lily. Place them on a board, folded side down to cool and firm. (Older recipes often suggest setting them pointed end down in small glasses or in the mesh of a wire cake cooler, but lying them down on a board works better for me. Whatever method you use, making these lilies is fairly fiddly …)

FINISHING

When you are ready to serve them, fill with a spoonful of whipped cream and place a strip of lemon jelly or peach in the centre of each cone. As a finishing touch, dust them with a little sifted icing sugar – and serve them forth. Makes about 24.

Portuguese Custard Tarts

FOR THE PASTRY CASES

1 batch	**cream cheese pastry, refrigerated overnight (see page 50)**	**1 batch**

FOR THE FILLING*

4	**egg yolks**	**4**
¼ cup	**caster sugar**	**50 g**
2 tbsp	**cornflour**	**20 g**
1 cup	**cream**	**250 ml**
½ cup	**water**	**125 ml**
a strip	**lemon rind**	**a strip**
2 tsp	**vanilla essence**	**2 tsp**

* **Lois Daish, the *New Zealand Listener*, 31 May 2003, page 41.**

I wanted to include a recipe for Portuguese Custard Tarts in the book and thought that the cream cheese pastry from the Apricot Crescents on page 50, although not traditional, might work well for them, too. So I made a test batch. Half the tarts had home-made rough puff pastry cases and the others had the cream cheese pastry. With Lois Daish's rich and creamy filling they couldn't help but taste very good, and my niece Aphra, who was working with me in the kitchen, agreed that the cream cheese pastry with its slight tang was the winner. These little tarts may not be particularly Portuguese, but they definitely are delicious.

GETTING READY

Preheat the oven to 400°F/200°C and remove the pastry from the fridge before you make the filling. Have ready a tray of 20 shallow patty tins or 12 muffin tins. There is no need to grease them.

MIXING AND BAKING

1. In a saucepan, whisk together the egg yolks, sugar and cornflour until well combined. Add the cream and water and keep whisking until the mixture is smooth.
2. Place over a medium heat, add the lemon rind and stir until the mixture comes to the boil. Remove from the heat immediately, remove the lemon rind, stir in the vanilla and set the custard aside to cool, stirring every now and then to prevent a skin from forming.
3. Roll out the pastry on a floured board to about ⅛ in/3 mm thickness and cut out rounds to fit your tins (experiment with a piece of tinfoil cut to size to ensure the pastry will come right up to the top of the tins). Reroll any scraps, placing them on top of each other to retain the layered structure of the pastry. Put the tray of pastry cases in the freezer for 5–10 minutes.
4. Spoon the cooled filling into the chilled cases and bake for 25 minutes, rotating the tray after 10 minutes. When they are done, the custard should have dark brown spots here and there. If they look a little pale you could turn on the grill for a few minutes, but watch them closely.
5. Remove from the oven, place on a rack to cool a little and, for the perfect taste and texture sensation, eat them while they are still warm.

Maple Walnut Cup Cakes

FOR THE CAKES

4 oz	butter	115 g
3 oz	caster sugar	85 g
2 tbsp	maple syrup	2 tbsp
½ tsp	vanilla essence	½ tsp
2	eggs	2
6 oz	flour	170 g
1 tsp	baking powder	1 tsp
¼ cup	milk	60 ml
3 oz	walnuts*	85 g

* finely chopped

FOR THE MAPLE SYRUP ICING

2 cups	icing sugar	240 g
4 oz	butter	115 g
2 tbsp	maple syrup	2 tbsp
2 tbsp	milk	2 tbsp
2 tbsp	walnuts*	25 g

* very finely chopped

NOTE

The elegant paper cases in this photograph came from a Japanese shop in Auckland. They are made from very firm waxed paper, hold their shape beautifully and are almost totally greaseproof. There are many sources of paper cases now so, although the pastel-coloured ones at the supermarket are still a good standby, you can also look further afield for variety.

It seems to me that in the recent enthusiasm for extravagantly decorated cup cakes, the flavour and texture of the cake itself often takes second place to the icing. The idea of a small cake is surely that the whole thing is enjoyable, not that you take one bite, eat a bit more of the icing, then leave the rest on your plate. My approach to cup cakes is this: make them small, make them tender and flavoursome – and make sure the icing complements the cake rather than overwhelms it. Here, then, is a recipe for some light, buttery cup cakes flavoured with maple syrup and walnuts, and crowned with a soft and creamy maple syrup icing.

GETTING READY

Preheat the oven to 350°F/180°C. Line 24 regular-sized patty tins or 36 tiny ones with paper cases. Bring the butter, eggs and milk to room temperature. Sift together the flour and baking powder.

MIXING AND BAKING

1. Cream the butter and sugar until soft and light (about 5 minutes with an electric beater). Beat in the maple syrup and the vanilla, then add the eggs one at a time, beating well after each addition.
2. Fold in the dry ingredients followed by the milk, then the walnuts.
3. Spoon into the paper cases and bake for about 20 minutes, rotating the tins after 10 minutes. They should be well risen and golden. Cool on a rack.

FINISHING

1. Make the icing by combining half the sifted icing sugar with the softened butter, maple syrup and milk and beating until smooth.
2. Add the remaining icing sugar gradually, beating well until the icing is a good spreading consistency. Spread or pipe it onto the cooled cakes and sprinkle with the walnuts. Makes 24 regular-sized or 36 tiny cup cakes.

Special Meringues

Most of my community cookbooks include at least one recipe for transforming leftover egg whites into small cakes that will keep well in the tin and are more substantial than ordinary meringues. The trick is to fold some extra ingredients into the meringue mix and many recipes suggest using breakfast cereals as well as dried fruit and nuts. On page 61 are three good possibilities.

Pictured, from left: Nut Kisses; Meringue Delights; Canadian Macaroons

INGREDIENTS FOR MIRACLE MERINGUES

1	**egg white**	**1**
1 cup	**caster sugar**	**200 g**
2 tbsp	**boiling water**	**30 ml**
1 tsp	**vinegar**	**1 tsp**
1 tsp	**baking powder**	**1 tsp**

***ETON MESS**

Eton Mess is made by gently folding coarsely crushed meringues and chopped strawberries (and/or other ripe berries) into softly whipped cream. A purée of berries drizzled on top is an optional extra.

MIRACLE MERINGUES

This is a way of stretching a single egg white to make three dozen miniature meringues – or 18 regular-sized ones – quite a feat, and most early cookery books have a version of this recipe. They are very white, have a slightly drier texture than regular meringues and crumble extremely well if you want to mix them with berries and cream for that famous English summer dessert, Eton Mess.* Marjorie Bond, one of the outstanding bakers at St Luke's Presbyterian Church in Auckland, kindly gave me her tried and true recipe.

GETTING READY

Preheat the oven to 300°F/150°C. Line two baking trays with baking paper, or grease them lightly and dust with flour. Have the egg white at room temperature.

MIXING AND BAKING

1. Put the egg white in the bowl of an electric mixer and cover it with the sugar. Pour on the boiling water and the vinegar and begin beating at high speed.
2. When the mixture is really thick and light (after about 7 minutes), add the baking powder and beat again.
3. Place teaspoonfuls on the prepared trays and bake for an hour. Remove to a rack to cool. Store airtight. Makes about 36 tiny meringues.

CANADIAN MACAROONS

From *Cooking For Fun*, Tokoroa, 1963, these are crisp and crunchy, right to the centre, and a lovely pale golden colour, thanks to the brown sugar.

2	**egg whites**	**2**
½ cup	**sugar**	**100 g**
½ cup	**brown sugar**	**100 g**
2 cups	**cornflakes**	**50 g**
1 cup	**desiccated coconut**	**85 g**
½ cup	**walnuts**	**50 g**
1 tbsp	**flour**	**1 tbsp**
½ tsp	**baking powder**	**½ tsp**
1 tsp	**vanilla essence**	**1 tsp**
¼ tsp	**almond essence**	**¼ tsp**

GETTING READY

Preheat the oven to 350°F/180°C. Line two trays with baking paper. Have the egg whites at room temperature. Chop the walnuts and combine with all the other dry ingredients except the white sugar.

MIXING AND BAKING

1. Whisk the egg whites until very stiff, then whisk in the white sugar a tablespoon at a time. Beat again until very stiff and glossy. Fold in the remaining dry ingredients with a metal spoon, followed by the essences.
2. Place teaspoonfuls on the trays and bake for 20 minutes, rotating the trays after 10 minutes. Cool on a rack and store airtight. Makes about 40.

MERINGUE DELIGHTS

From the 1939 New Zealand Women's Institutes *Home Cookery Book*, these are crisp on the outside and slightly chewy inside. They are cooked for an hour at a low temperature, then left overnight in the turned-off oven.

2	**egg whites**	**2**
6 tbsp	**sugar**	**90 g**
6	**glacé cherries**	**6**
¼ cup	**walnuts**	**25 g**
¼ cup	**raisins**	**35 g**
1 tsp	**vinegar**	**1 tsp**
1 cup	**cornflakes**	**25 g**

GETTING READY

Preheat the oven to 260°F/130°C. Line two trays with baking paper. Have the egg whites at room temperature. Chop the cherries, walnuts and raisins.

MIXING AND BAKING

1. Whisk the egg whites until very stiff, then fold in the sugar slowly and gently with a metal spoon. Add the cherries, walnuts, raisins, and vinegar and lastly the cornflakes.
2. Put dessertspoonfuls of the mixture on the trays and bake for an hour, then turn off the oven, open the door slightly and leave them there overnight to dry out. Store airtight. Makes about 30.

NUT KISSES

From *Tried Recipes*, published by the 'Ever Ready Committee' of the Victoria League, Auckland, circa 1925, these are chewy rather than crisp. The recipe's contributor was Mrs Alfrey of Mt Eden.

1	**egg white**	**1**
¼ tsp	**salt**	**¼ tsp**
1 cup	**icing sugar**	**120 g**
½ tsp	**vanilla essence**	**½ tsp**
30	**dates**	**120 g**
1 cup	**walnuts**	**100 g**
2 oz	**chocolate***	**55 g**

*** The chocolate is my addition and can be left out if you wish.**

GETTING READY

Preheat the oven to 290°F/140°C. Line two trays with baking paper. Have the egg white at room temperature and sift the icing sugar. Chop the dates into small pieces, then chop them again with the walnuts and the chocolate.

MIXING AND BAKING

1. Whisk the egg white and salt until stiff, then beat in the icing sugar a tablespoon at a time. Keep beating for a minute or two, then fold in the remaining ingredients.
2. Put dessertspoonfuls of the mixture on the trays and bake for 30 minutes, rotating after 20 minutes. Cool on a rack. Store airtight. Makes about 24.

Harmony Tarts and Matrimony Tarts

FOR THE PASTRY

¼ cup	butter	55 g
¼ cup	sugar	50 g
1	egg yolk	1
1 cup*	flour	170 g
½ tsp	baking powder	½ tsp
1–2 tbsp	milk	1–2 tbsp

* large cup

FILLING AND TOPPING FOR HARMONY TARTS

1	egg white	1
¼ cup	sugar	50 g
¼ cup	desiccated coconut	25 g
1 tsp	lemon zest*	1 tsp
4 tbsp	raspberry jam	4 tbsp

* finely grated

FILLING AND TOPPING FOR MATRIMONY TARTS

1	egg white	1
¼ cup	sugar	50 g
¼ cup	ground almonds	30 g
4 tbsp	apricot jam	4 tbsp
1 tbsp	currants	1 tbsp
2 tbsp	flaked almonds*	2 tbsp

* optional

Harmony Tarts appear in many early cookbooks and their very harmonious combination of tender, buttery pastry, a dab of raspberry jam and some lemony coconut meringue has never lost its appeal. They are a bit like Louise Cake, but with the added charm of being a small, self-contained package. Matrimony Tarts are a variation on the theme, with a filling of apricot jam and a few currants under an almond topping. You could bake a batch of each and create a highly desirable pairing.

GETTING READY

Preheat the oven to 375°F/190°C. Bring the butter and egg to room temperature, sift together the flour and baking powder, and stir the jam to loosen it. Have ready 12 ungreased shallow patty tins.

MIXING AND BAKING

1. Cream the butter and sugar until soft and light. Add the egg yolk followed by the dry ingredients, adding the milk if you need it to make a firm dough. (You can make this pastry very easily in the food processor.) Form the dough into a flat disc, wrap in waxed paper and refrigerate for 10 minutes to firm it a little.
2. Roll out the dough on a lightly floured board and cut out rounds to fit your tins, with fluted or plain edges as you prefer. Chill the cases for another 10 minutes and prepare the filling.
3. Whisk the egg white until stiff, beat in the sugar a little at a time, then fold in the coconut and lemon zest for the Harmony Tarts, or the ground almonds for Matrimony Tarts. You could also add a drop of almond essence if you wish.
4. Put a small teaspoonful of jam in the bottom of each tartlet case, but don't use too much or it will bubble out and burn. Drop a few currants on top of the apricot jam for Matrimony Tarts. Spoon on the topping, leaving the pastry edges visible, and sprinkle either with a little more desiccated coconut, or a few flaked almonds for Matrimony Tarts.
5. Bake until the topping is light brown and toasted and the pastry edges are golden – about 20 minutes, rotating after 10 minutes. Cool on a rack in the tins for about 15 minutes, then loosen the tarts very gently with a round-bladed table knife, remove from the tins and cool thoroughly. Sift over a little icing sugar, or serve with a spoonful of whipped cream on top if you wish. Makes 12.

Sponge Kisses or Powder Puffs

FOR THE CAKES

2	eggs	2
4 oz	caster sugar	115 g
3 oz	flour	85 g
1 tsp	baking powder	1 tsp
pinch	salt	pinch
4 tbsp	caster sugar, extra	4 tbsp

FOR THE FILLING AND TO FINISH

1 cup	cream	225 ml
3–4 tbsp	jam	3–4 tbsp
	icing sugar, for dusting	

New Zealand Country Women's Institutes Cookery Book, 1955 reprint. In her foreword, Dominion President E. M. Martin writes, 'Both the experienced and the inexperienced housewife will be assured of success with the excellent recipes contained in the issue.' And the page is headed: 'If you know a good thing, pass it on.'

Among the hardest to resist of all, these are small, crisp sponge cakes that soften deliciously when filled with jam and whipped cream. You can store them in a tin for several weeks and, as long as you fill them three or four hours before serving them, they will have a tender, freshly baked texture. They are in most cookery books and I have always used the recipe in my mother Paula's copy of the 1945 Women's Institutes *Home Cookery Book*, where they are called Sponge Drops.

GETTING READY

Preheat the oven to 425°F/215°C and line two baking trays with baking paper or greased greaseproof paper. (You do need paper of some kind as you'll be sifting sugar over the cakes before they bake and it would fuse onto the baking trays.) Bring the eggs to room temperature. Sift together the flour, baking powder and salt – twice.

MIXING AND BAKING

1. Beat the eggs until pale with an electric beater, then add the first measure of caster sugar a tablespoon at a time, beating steadily until the mixture is thick and falls in ribbons from the beaters when you lift them out (about 9 minutes).
2. Sift the dry ingredients (except for the extra sugar) on to the mixture and fold gently through with a shallow metal spoon.
3. Drop small circular spoonfuls on the prepared trays. Try to keep them all the same size as you want to pair them up later. Dropping the mixture from the tip of the spoon, rather than the side, helps with this, or you could use a forcing bag with a 1 cm opening and pipe out small mounds. Sift caster sugar over the tops of the cakes and bake for 5–6 minutes until risen and golden, but not brown. Leave on the tray for 4–5 minutes before removing to a rack to finish cooling. Store airtight.

FINISHING

1. About 3–5 hours before you intend to serve them, pair up the cakes and put them together with a little jam and a generous spoonful of whipped cream. Some recipes for Powder Puffs suggest tinting the mixture pink with a little food colouring before you bake the cakes, and folding the jam into the whipped cream so it is pink, too.
2. Sift some icing sugar onto a sheet of waxed paper on an oven tray. Arrange the cakes in a single layer and dust them with more icing sugar, then set aside in a cool place to soften.
3. Pile onto a pretty plate with a doily and wait for the compliments to flow. Makes 18 large or 36 tiny kisses.

Larger Cakes –
Plain and Fancy

Although they should always look appetising and smell wonderful, large cakes can meet quite different domestic and social needs. There are those that you keep safely in a tin and then produce a slice or two at opportune moments; those that you present with a flourish – to be greeted with applause – on those special occasions when a fancier cake is called for; and then there is the cake made at the last minute and eaten warm at home, or on a picnic or car journey.

The range of cakes in this chapter covers all these requirements. All have been well tested on my family and friends, who have accorded them choruses of approval. None of them involves complicated or tricky processes and I trust that you and your family will enjoy making them – and eating them, of course.

Crunchy Topped Lemon Loaf

FOR THE CAKE

¼ lb	**butter**	**115 g**
¾ cup	**caster sugar**	**150 g**
2 tsp	**lemon zest***	**2 tsp**
2	**eggs**	**2**
1½ cups	**flour**	**180 g**
1 tsp	**baking powder**	**1 tsp**
½ cup	**milk**	**110 ml**

***finely grated**

FOR THE TOPPING

⅓ cup	**caster sugar**	**70 g**
2 tbsp	**lemon juice**	**2 tbsp**

Myra Lawrie is a wonderful cake baker, but not a great cake eater, so her family and many friends are the fortunate beneficiaries of her skill in the kitchen. When she gave me this recipe, however, she described the cake as 'lovely', and said, 'Even *I* will eat it!' The recipe came from her older sister Nancy Yarndley – another wonderful baker – who shares Myra's lack of a sweet tooth. In her version of this popular lemon loaf cake with a crunchy sugar and lemon juice topping, Nancy has reduced the sugar quantities to give the cake an intense lemony tang – and it has a very soft, fine crumb. It keeps well in an airtight tin and freezes beautifully.

GETTING READY

Preheat the oven to 350°F/180°C. Lightly grease a medium-sized (8½ x 4½ in/22 x 11 cm) loaf tin and line the bottom with a rectangle of baking paper. Bring the butter and eggs to room temperature. Sift together the flour and baking powder.

MIXING AND BAKING

1. Cream the butter and sugar until light and fluffy, beat in the lemon zest, then add the eggs one at a time, beating well after each addition.
2. Use a metal spoon to gently fold in the dry ingredients in about three lots, alternating with the milk.
3. Pour the mixture into the prepared tin, smooth the top and bake for about 40 minutes, rotating halfway through. The cake will be a beautiful golden brown with a long crack running along the top and should be just pulling away from the sides of the tin. Remove from the oven and place on a cooling rack, still in the tin.

FINISHING

For the topping combine the sugar and lemon juice in a small bowl, then spoon the mixture over the top of the still-hot cake. It will soak in a little and run down the sides, leaving a thin crust of sugar on the top. Finish cooling in the tin, then turn out carefully. Store airtight. If you are going to freeze the cake, cool it completely and wrap well in waxed paper and aluminium foil first.

Mollie Newell's Ginger Cake

INGREDIENTS

2 cups*	**flour**	**300 g**
1 cup**	**sugar**	**150 g**
1 tsp	**baking powder**	**1 tsp**
1 tsp	**baking soda**	**1 tsp**
1 dsp	**ground ginger**	**2 tsp**
½ tsp	**mixed spice**	**½ tsp**
½ tsp	**cinnamon**	**½ tsp**
2	**eggs**	**2**
1 cup**	**milk**	**200 ml**
½ lb	**butter**	**225 g**
1 cup**	**golden syrup**	**275 g**

* **breakfast cups**
** **teacup**

Mollie Newell was another of Myra Lawrie's sisters – eldest of the six girls who grew up on farms near Levin and Te Awamutu, the daughters of Norman and Selina Verity. The sisters were keen cooks and as adults kept each other supplied with good recipes for more than 60 years. Mollie's particular specialities were Christmas cake and this buttery ginger cake. A cup of tea with Myra, who is now in her mid-80s, is invariably accompanied by a piece of her outstanding shortbread and an animated discussion of the merits of some new recipe and whether or not the results of her testing are all that she hoped. Ginger Cake, like the Lemon Loaf on page 68, meets her stringent quality requirements and is also very easily made. As usual, I agree with Myra – it is a winner.

GETTING READY

Preheat the oven to 350°F/180°C. Grease and flour two loaf tins or a large ring tin. You could also make it in a small roasting dish. Heat the butter and golden syrup gently and stir until the butter is melted.

MIXING AND BAKING

1. Put the flour, sugar and all the other dry ingredients into a large mixing bowl and combine thoroughly (I use a metal whisk for this). In another bowl, beat the eggs, mix in the milk, then tip them into the dry ingredients and mix lightly.
2. Add the butter and golden syrup and stir everything thoroughly together to make a smooth, fairly runny batter.
3. Tip it into the prepared tins and bake for 45 minutes, rotating after 30 minutes. Remove from the oven when the cake smells cooked and springs back when you push the centre gently with your finger. Leave it to cool on a rack for at least 15 minutes before turning out of the tin. Store airtight.

A NOTE ON CAKE TINS

Mollie always made this cake in two loaf tins, but I used a fluted ring tin, which produces a cake of about the same thickness. I measured the volume of my tin in cups of water and compared that with the capacity of a pair of loaf tins. If you don't have exactly the size of tin stipulated in a recipe, you can usually make some adjustments – even bake extra mixture in a couple of muffin tins. Myra chooses to make this in a roasting dish, then cuts it into four slabs – some to keep and some to give away.

Ginger Cake
ix dry ingredients –
breakfast cups flour
tea cup sugar
teaspoon Baking powder
" " " Soda
desertspoon groundginger
teaspoon each of spice
& cinnamon.

dd 2 well beaten
ggs 1 teacup Golden
Syrup 1 teacup milk
½ lb melted butter

ake ¾ hour – oven
at 350° F. 180°C
just buttered then
floured the tin
& cooked it in

Quarg Fruit Cake

INGREDIENTS

6½ oz	butter	185 g
1½ cups	caster sugar	300 g
3 tsp	fennel seeds*	3 tsp
9 oz	quarg	250 g
2 tsp	lemon zest**	2 tsp
4	eggs	4
2 cups	flour	250 g
2 tsp	baking powder	2 tsp
6 oz	golden sultanas†	170 g
4 oz	dried pears	115 g
4 oz	dried apricots	115 g
2 oz	pine nuts	55 g

* optional, but a delicious and aromatic addition

** finely grated

† The original recipe just says 'mixed fruit and nuts', so as long as you have 16 oz/455 g total weight, you can use any combination you like. Crystallised ginger, walnuts and raisins make a good one.

Quarg – or quark, or kvark – is an ancient type of soft, fresh cheese made from skimmed milk and particularly popular in Germany. A commercially made version appeared in New Zealand around 1985 and with it came a small leaflet of recipes, including this one. I remember visiting my friend Bridget Ikin about this time and finding her making the cake, which turned out extremely well. I'm very grateful to Bridget since I was unlikely to have tried the recipe but, once I did, I began making it often, experimenting with flavours and different combinations of fruit and nuts. Quarg seems no longer to be available here, so I make the cake with *fromage frais* or ricotta and still get excellent results, but the name has stayed. As Alan Davidson says in *The Oxford Companion to Food*, 'The growing popularity of quark outside Germany is perhaps partly due to its name; to non-German ears, this is memorable, faintly mysterious, and suggestive of an invention by Lewis Carroll.'‡ Or maybe Dr Seuss?

GETTING READY

Preheat the oven to 300°F/150°C. Grease an 8 in/20 cm deep, round cake tin and line it with two layers of baking paper. Bring the butter and eggs to room temperature, put the sugar in a food processor or blender with 2 tsp of the fennel seeds and whiz for about half a minute. The seeds will still look whole, but the sugar will now be fennel-scented. Sift the flour and baking powder together, and chop the dried pears and apricots into small pieces.

MIXING AND BAKING

1. Cream the butter and fennel-seedy sugar until soft and light (this takes at least 5 minutes), then beat in the quarg, fromage frais or ricotta and the lemon zest. The mixture will curdle, but don't worry.
2. Beat in the eggs one at time, then gently fold in the dry ingredients. The batter will now be smooth and creamy. Mix in the fruit and nuts.
3. Put the mixture into the prepared tin, level the top and sprinkle with the remaining teaspoon of fennel seeds. Bake for about 2 hours, rotating the tin after an hour. The cake must be cooked slowly to prevent the top from cracking too much but if you need to, raise the temperature slightly at the end to brown the top.
4. Cool on a rack in the tin for at least 30 minutes before turning it out. Store airtight. This cake keeps very well and the flavour goes on improving for a week or so, but it is also good served slightly warm.

‡ *Alan Davidson, The Oxford Companion to Food, Oxford University Press, 1999, page 644.*

QUARG

Although there are hundreds of German recipes using quarg – particularly for cheesecakes and pastries – I haven't come across any for this kind of fruit cake. There may perhaps be a connection with those American cakes made in decorative circular Bundt pans – similar to Gugelhupf moulds – with sour cream or yoghurt in the batter. These cakes are light and moist and without the heaviness that extra butter would give them. So this quarg cake feels like a hybrid – an English fruit cake made with German cheese in an American style, and the fennel seed and pine nut version I've given here always tastes slightly Italian to me. Whatever its provenance, it is a very good recipe.

Picnic Berry Cake

INGREDIENTS

3½ oz	butter	100 g
7 oz	caster sugar	200 g
1	egg	1
½ tsp	vanilla essence	½ tsp
8 oz	flour	220 g
2 tsp	baking powder	2 tsp
⅔ cup	milk	150 ml
5½ oz	fruit	150 g
2-3 tbsp	caster sugar, extra	2-3 tbsp

Sometimes it is nice to have a cake that is made with fresh fruit and can be eaten warm, almost like a pie. This lovely cake is from Lois Daish's *New Zealand Listener* column of 15 January 1990. She wrote: 'This recipe is loosely derived from one in an English fundraising cookbook published to raise money for kitchen improvements at the village hall in Lavant, near Chichester. The hall, like so many in New Zealand, was built as a memorial after World War I. The recipe is for a plain cake studded with fresh berries – blackcurrants in the original recipe, and heavily sprinkled with sugar before baking to make a light crust. It may be carried hot in the tin to a picnic, and is still moist and good to eat two days later.' Lois suggests blackcurrants, blueberries or chopped fresh apricots as possibilities and I recently made it with frozen blackcurrants, stewed quinces and little lumps of home-made quince paste. So the choice of fruit is up to you. For the cake in the photograph I used chopped Omega plums and scattered a few slivered almonds on top, under the sugar.

GETTING READY

Preheat the oven to 350°F/180°C. Grease and flour an 8 in/20 cm round or square shallow tin. Bring the butter and egg to room temperature and sift together the flour and baking powder. If you are using fresh summer fruit, other than berries, chop it into smallish chunks. (You don't need to thaw frozen berries before adding them to the cake.)

MIXING AND BAKING

1. Cream the butter and sugar until soft and light. Beat in the egg and vanilla, then fold in the dry ingredients alternately with the milk.
2. Gently stir in the berries or fruit, then scoop the mixture into the tin. Sprinkle the top generously with the extra sugar and bake for about 40 minutes, rotating after 25 minutes. Serve straight from the tin.

Sister Blake's Cake

This is another of the 16 recipes that Shirley Dunphy contributed to the 1963 Tokoroa fundraising recipe book, *Cooking for Fun*. (The Chocolate Caramel Fingers in *Ladies, a Plate* were also hers.) Sister Blake was the nursing sister who set up a maternity service for Tokoroa in the 1950s with the help of Sister Bell and Shirley, a young nurse at the time. Tokoroa was then a busy timber town, bursting with young families, and the dedication and hard work of these three women ensured that its new mothers were well cared for – in the three small suburban houses which were made available to them. Sister Blake's Cake is a simple wholemeal shortcake with a smooth date filling which has real charm and keeps getting better every time you cut a piece.

INGREDIENTS

4 oz	**butter**	**115 g**
4 oz	**sugar**	**115 g**
1 tbsp	**golden syrup**	**25 g**
1	**egg**	**1**
1 cup*	**wholemeal flour**	**150 g**
1 tsp**	**baking powder**	**¾ tsp**
pinch	**salt**	**pinch**
1 cup	**dates†**	**120 g**
6 tbsp	**water**	**6 tbsp**
½ tsp	**vanilla essence**	**½ tsp**

* big cup
** small tsp
† chopped

GETTING READY

Preheat the oven to 350°F/180°C. Grease a shallow 8 in/20 cm round tin and line the base with a piece of baking paper. Bring the butter and egg to room temperature and mix together the flour and baking powder. Simmer the dates for a few minutes with the water until very soft and flavour with the vanilla. Set aside to cool.

MIXING AND BAKING

1. Cream the butter and sugar until soft and light, then add the golden syrup. Beat in the egg, then mix in the dry ingredients.
2. Spread half the mixture in the tin, cover with the cooled dates, then put the remaining mixture on top. Spread it out as evenly as you can.
3. Bake for about 25 minutes, rotating halfway through. It should be well risen and golden brown. Cool on a rack in the tin for at least 15 minutes before turning out carefully. Store airtight.

Arabian Spice Cake

FOR THE CAKE

4 oz	butter	115 g
1 cup	caster sugar	200 g
2 tbsp	golden syrup	2 tbsp
2	eggs	2
1½ tsp	mixed spice	1½ tsp
2 cups	flour	250 g
2 tsp	baking powder	2 tsp
½ cup	milk	115 ml

FOR THE APRICOT GLAZE

4 oz	apricot jam	15 g
2 tbsp	water	2 tbsp
2 tbsp	rum or brandy*	2 tbsp

* optional

FOR THE ARABIAN FILLING

5 oz	butter	140 g
5 tbsp	strong coffee	75 ml
1½ tsp	vanilla essence	1½ tsp
3 tbsp	cocoa	3 tbsp
3½ cups	icing sugar	420 g

FOR THE COFFEE GLACÉ ICING

1 cup	icing sugar	120 g
4 tsp	strong coffee	20 ml

FOR THE SIDES

4 oz	flaked almonds	115 g

Earlier this year, in one of my favourite secondhand book shops – Dunedin's Octagon Books – I found the *St Paul's Cookery Book*, published in 1956 by the Women's Fellowship of St Paul's Presbyterian Church, Oamaru. It is a treasure chest of excellent recipes and the Arabian Spice Cake was contributed by V.M. Proctor. I had been looking for just such a recipe because a friend, Tim Walker, had named this as the cake he and his sisters always asked for on their birthdays. I'm not surprised. It is a deliciously tender spice cake with an 'Arabian' filling of mocha butter icing flavoured with cocoa and strong coffee (this is not the place for coffee essence). To make it into a cake for a very special occasion I have cut it into four layers, added an apricot jam glaze, pressed toasted almonds around the sides and put a layer of coffee glacé icing on the top. Despite all this embellishment, it still slices well and tastes as good as it looks.

GETTING READY

Preheat the oven to 350°F/180°C. While the oven is heating toast the flaked almonds in a shallow tray for about 5 minutes until golden. Grease two 8 in/20 cm shallow sponge sandwich tins, line the bases with rounds of baking paper, grease the paper and flour the inside of the tins. Bring the butter, eggs and milk to room temperature and sift together the flour and baking powder. Beat the eggs with a fork and add the mixed spice. Make the apricot glaze by heating together the jam, water and rum or brandy, if using, until slightly thickened. Strain into a bowl and set aside.

MIXING AND BAKING

1. Cream the butter and sugar until soft and light, then add the golden syrup. Pour in the egg and spice mixture in two lots, beating well after each addition. Fold in the dry ingredients alternately with the milk, then divide the mixture evenly between the two tins.
2. Bake for 30 minutes, rotating the tins after 20 minutes. The cakes should be just pulling away from the sides of the tins. Cool on a rack, then turn out after 15 minutes to cool completely. Split each cake in half horizontally with a long serrated knife using a sawing motion.

FINISHING

1. For the filling, cream the softened butter with the coffee, vanilla, sifted cocoa and half the sifted icing sugar. When well combined, add the remainder of the icing sugar and beat until you have a soft, creamy consistency.
2. Put the bottom layer of cake onto a sheet of card or the base of a flan tin and spread thinly with the filling. Repeat with the other layers, leaving the top plain. Put the remaining filling in a small bowl and cover with a damp cloth.
3. Warm the apricot glaze slightly and brush a thin coat over the top and sides of the cake. Set aside for about 30 minutes until the glaze is set.
4. Spread a thin layer of the Arabian filling over the sides of the cake and press the flaked almonds onto this with the flat of your hand, catching those that fall on a clean plate. Keep going until the sides are well encrusted with almonds.
5. Put the rest of the Arabian filling into a paper forcing bag (see page 10) with a star nozzle and pipe a rim of stars around the top of the cake. This will prevent the coffee icing from flowing down the sides. Chill the cake for about 15 minutes.
6. To make the icing, sift the icing sugar into a heatproof bowl, or the top of a double boiler, mix in the coffee to make a smooth, thick mixture and set the bowl over simmering water, stirring with a wooden spoon. It will very quickly soften and become quite runny. Pour it quickly on top of the cake and let it spread out to the edge. (You could pipe a message on the top in melted chocolate, or decorate the cake with another Arabian star in the centre.) Carefully lift the cake onto a pretty serving dish, make a cup of tea, sit down and enjoy your creation.

Chocaroon Cake

FOR THE CAKE

3 oz	**butter**	**85 g**
4 oz	**sugar**	**115 g**
1 tsp	**lemon zest***	**1 tsp**
½ tsp	**vanilla essence**	**½ tsp**
2	**egg yolks**	**2**
6 oz	**self-raising flour†**	**170 g**
1 cup	**milk**	**225 ml**
2 tsp	**jam**	**2 tbsp**

* finely grated
† or use plain flour and 1½ tsp baking powder

FOR THE CHOCAROON LAYER

2	**egg whites**	**2**
2 tbsp	**sugar**	**30 g**
½ cup	**desiccated coconut**	**40 g**
1 tbsp	**cocoa**	**1 tbsp**
	icing sugar, for dusting	

One of my favourite community cookbooks, simply called *Our Recipe Book*, was published in December 1967 by the Karitane Public Hall Building Committee. It has an interesting selection of recipes and as soon as I saw this one with its promising name and its baked-in filling and topping I knew I had to try it. At the end of the recipe Mrs L. Stewart, who contributed it to the book, noted: 'This recipe won $10 in a recipe contest.' More than 40 years ago $10 was a much more significant amount than it seems today, and the cake is so pretty and delicious it certainly deserved its prize.

GETTING READY

Preheat the oven to 350°F/180°C. Lightly grease a medium-sized (8½ x 4½ in/22 x 11 cm) loaf tin and line the bottom with a rectangle of baking paper. Bring the butter, eggs and milk to room temperature. Sift the flour, with the baking powder if using it.

MIXING AND BAKING

1. Make the Chocaroon mixture first. Whisk the egg whites until stiff, then gradually beat in the sugar. Fold in the coconut and the sifted cocoa. Set aside.
2. Cream the butter and sugar until soft and light, then beat in the lemon zest and vanilla. Add the egg yolks and beat well. Fold in the flour alternately with the milk to make a soft batter.
3. Spoon half the mixture into the prepared tin, followed by half the Chocaroon mixture, spread out as evenly as possible. Top with the remaining cake mixture and spread this lightly with the jam. (The jam just helps the topping adhere to the cake, so it needn't be a thick layer; I used the apricot glaze on page 76.) Top with the remaining Chocaroon mixture.
4. Bake for 45–50 minutes or until the cake is pulling away from the sides of the tin. Cool in the tin, then turn out very carefully. A paper towel on top of the cake when you turn it out will contain any loose coconut. Sift a little icing sugar over before serving the cake in neat slices.

Chocolate Cream Sponge

FOR THE CAKE

3	eggs	3
pinch	salt	pinch
4 oz	caster sugar	115 g
3 oz	flour	85 g
½ tsp	baking powder	½ tsp
¾ oz	cocoa	3 tbsp
4 tbsp	milk	4 tbsp
½ tsp	vanilla essence	½ tsp

FOR THE FILLING

2 oz	butter	55 g
4 tbsp	icing sugar	65 g
4 tsp	brandy	4 tsp
1–2 tsp	hot water	1–2 tsp
3–4 tbsp	strawberry jam	3–4 tbsp
	icing sugar, for dusting	

A chocolate sponge filled with whipped cream – or even a buttery mock cream – and jam, of course, will always be welcome on the afternoon tea table. This tender sponge is from Margaret Bates's 1964 book, *Talking about Cakes with an Irish and Scottish Accent*, and is made with Miss Bates's preferred whisking method for sponges. She starts by beating the egg whites until stiff, then adds the yolks and the sugar alternately before folding in the flour. This makes the beating much easier if you are doing it with a hand beater or whisk, and I often use her method with an electric mixer, too. I've filled this one with strawberry jam and brandy-flavoured mock cream, and used a paper doily as a stencil for the icing sugar sifted on top.

GETTING READY

Preheat the oven to 400°F/200°C. Grease two 8 in/20 cm shallow, round sponge sandwich tins. Line the base of the tins with rounds of baking paper, grease the paper and flour the insides of the tins. Bring the eggs to room temperature and sift together the flour and baking powder. Mix together the cocoa and milk in a small bowl until they form a smooth cream (this takes a few minutes). Separate the eggs.

MIXING AND BAKING

1. Whisk the egg whites with the salt until stiff. Gradually beat in the caster sugar and the egg yolks one at a time, whisking well after each addition. After at least 10 minutes of whisking you should have a pale lemon-coloured, light and spongy mixture.
2. Gently mix in the sifted dry ingredients, the cocoa cream and the vanilla, lifting and folding until the marbled streaks have all gone and the mixture is a uniform milk-chocolate colour.
3. Spoon carefully into the prepared tins, tilting the tins to even out the mixture, and bake for 15–20 minutes. Turn out with care once they have cooled for a few minutes.

FINISHING

Make the mock cream by beating the softened butter, sifted icing sugar and the brandy for several minutes, then add the hot water a little at a time and keep beating until the mixture is light and fluffy. Spread the lower half of the cake with the mock cream, top with small spoonfuls of jam and put on the top layer. Dredge with icing sugar before serving.

A ROYAL SPONGE

After the 1953–54 Royal Tour of New Zealand, cakes with this name began appearing in many community cookbooks. Lois Daish gave the explanation in her *New Zealand Listener* column of 12 July 1986. It seems that Queen Elizabeth II commented on a piece of chocolate cake she had been given at a Plunket Society afternoon tea in Dunedin. She later described it as 'really delicious. It was a chocolate cake made with peppermint icing and cream filling.' The cake had been made by Mrs Jessie Deaker, a member of the Dominion Executive of the society, and for many years afterwards Mrs Deaker made dozens of the renamed Royal Sponges to sell on Plunket's annual fundraising day. This chocolate sponge is not exactly the same as Mrs Deaker's, but if you ice it with a thin layer of peppermint-flavoured icing made with icing sugar and melted butter, and top that with chocolate butter icing and grated chocolate, you will be eating (almost) the cake the Queen ate.

Ladysmith Cake

INGREDIENTS

6½ oz	butter	185 g
6½ oz	sugar	185 g
1 tsp	vanilla essence	1 tsp
3	eggs	3
6½ oz	flour	185 g
1 tbsp	cornflour	15 g
1 tsp	baking powder	1 tsp
1 tsp	ground cinnamon	1 tsp
1 tsp	mixed spice*	1 tsp
4 tbsp	jam**	4 tbsp
½ cup	walnuts	50 g

* Some recipes suggest using cocoa rather than mixed spice. I prefer spice.
** raspberry, strawberry or blackcurrant

The Southland Patriotic Cookery Book: In Aid of Patriotic Funds, 1940 was compiled by Flora M. Crawford and Mary I. Lousley and published in Invercargill. This copy was lent to me by Dorothy and Ian McCarrison.

Ladysmith Cake celebrates the lifting of the four-month siege of the South African town of Ladysmith in February 1900 – a milestone in the Boer War and a cause for rejoicing throughout the British Empire. The cake seems to be a New Zealand invention and recipes for it appear in many early twentieth-century community cookbooks. This excellent version, made with equal weights of eggs, butter, sugar and flour, was contributed by Mrs Hugh Carswell to *The Southland Patriotic Cookery Book: In Aid of Patriotic Funds*, published in Invercargill in 1940. Half the mixture is flavoured with spices, put in the cake tin and spread with jam; the remaining mixture goes on the top and is sprinkled with chopped walnuts before baking. Ladysmith Cake deserves to be made and enjoyed today since it looks pretty, cuts and keeps well – and it tastes delightful.

GETTING READY

Preheat the oven to 350°F/180°C. Grease a 7 in/18 cm square cake tin and line the base and two sides of the tin with a strip of baking paper. Sift together the flour, cornflour and baking powder. Coarsely chop the walnuts.

MIXING AND BAKING

1. Cream the butter and sugar until light and fluffy, beat in the vanilla, then add the eggs one at a time, beating well after each addition.
2. Carefully fold in the sifted dry ingredients until the mixture is smooth. Scoop half the mixture into another bowl, sift the spices on top, gently fold them through, then spread the mixture evenly in the prepared cake tin.
3. Spoon the jam onto the spicy cake mixture in the tin and spread it out as evenly as you can, then top with the remaining plain cake mixture. Sprinkle the chopped walnuts over.
4. Bake for 50–60 minutes, rotating the cake after 30 minutes, until the top springs back when pressed lightly.
5. Remove from the oven and cool in the tin on a rack for about 10 minutes. Put a clean cloth or a paper towel on top of the cake (to hold the walnuts) and turn out onto another wire rack. Invert onto the first rack, remove the towel and leave to cool. Store in an airtight tin and serve in small – or generous – slices.

Sir Edmund Hillary's Birthday Cake

FOR THE CAKE

13 oz	butter	370 g
4½ cups	caster sugar	900 g
6	eggs	6
6 cups	flour	750 g
3 tsp	baking powder	3 tsp
1 tsp	baking soda	1 tsp
½ tsp	salt	½ tsp
3 cups*	mashed banana	3 cups
2 tbsp	lemon juice	2 tbsp
12 tbsp	milk	180 ml
3 tsp	vanilla essence	3 tsp

* about 6 bananas

FOR THE FILLING AND ICING

½ pint	cream*	300 ml
1	banana	1
2 cups	icing sugar	240 g
2-3 tbsp	lemon juice	2-3 tbsp
⅓ cup	extra cream**	100 ml
3½ oz	dark chocolate**	100 g

* whipped
** for the chocolate ganache

NOTE

If you want a less gigantic cake, make one-third of the mixture and bake it in an 8 in/21 cm round tin.

For Sir Edmund Hillary's 80th birthday his daughter Sarah asked me if I would make a dessert cake for the family dinner at her house. I was pleased and honoured to be asked and suggested a hazelnut meringue cake with an apricot filling and a topping of suitably mountainous-looking whipped cream. According to Sarah it was a great success. But in 1999 I had no idea that six years on I would be the curator of an exhibition about Sir Edmund's life and achievements, and would have just finished writing his biography. So for his 86th birthday, on 20 July 2005, having got to know Ed a little better, I made the kind of simple cake that was his favourite – and a popular choice with many New Zealanders. It is a very large, very tender banana cake with a filling of whipped cream and sliced bananas and a shiny, lemon-flavoured glacé icing. Ed loved it and I think you will, too.

GETTING READY

Preheat the oven to 325°F/160°C. Grease a 12 in/30 cm round cake tin, at least 3 in/8 cm deep, and line the base with a circle of baking paper. Bring the butter and eggs to room temperature, sift together the flour, baking powder and soda and salt, and add the lemon juice to the milk and set it aside to sour.

MIXING AND BAKING

1. Cream the butter and sugar until soft and light. Add the eggs one at a time, beating well after each addition. I do this in a food mixer, then transfer the creamed mixture to a very large bowl.
2. Add the dry ingredients alternately with the mashed bananas and the soured milk. Use one hand to add the ingredients and the other to fold them in; the mixture is too heavy to manage with a spoon. Lastly add the vanilla.
3. Use your hand to scoop the mixture into the prepared tin, level the top and bake for about 90 minutes, rotating the tin after an hour. The cake rises very evenly and has a nice flat top for icing. Cool on a wire rack (this takes more than an hour).

FINISHING

1. Split the cake horizontally with a long, serrated knife. Put the lower half on a serving platter and spread with the whipped cream. Top with thinly sliced banana, then the other half of the cake.
2. Sift the icing sugar into a heatproof bowl, or the top of a double boiler, mix in the lemon juice to make a smooth, thick mixture and set the bowl over simmering water, stirring the icing with a wooden spoon. It will very quickly soften and become quite runny. Pour it over the cake, allowing it to dribble down the sides a little.
3. Make the chocolate ganache for decorating the top of the cake by bringing the cream to the boil and pouring it onto the chopped chocolate in a bowl. Stir until the chocolate melts and the mixture is smooth and glossy. Let it sit for about 20 minutes then, when it has thickened a little, use a paper forcing bag to pipe your message. (See page 10 for instructions on making a forcing bag.) Keep the cake in a cool place and serve within 4 or 5 hours of filling and decorating. Even if you can fit it in your fridge, chilling it makes the ganache and the glacé icing lose their shine.

Items to be Buttered

I always think that this section in the community cookbooks is the closest we get to seeing what people really liked to eat in earlier years. Spreading something with butter just before it is eaten takes us back to basics – to hot toast for breakfast, scones or pikelets for morning tea and a slice of fruit loaf in the afternoon. Not necessarily every day, but fairly often and certainly at weekends.

This selection of recipes includes a number that I have made for years and a couple of recent discoveries that have quickly proved to be irresistible. Bake some of the items from this chapter regularly, become familiar with the recipes and pass them on to family and friends. All are easily made – and very easily eaten.

Banana Nut Loaf

INGREDIENTS

3	ripe bananas*	3
2	eggs	2
¾ cup	sugar	150 g
2 cups	flour	250 g
1 tsp	salt	1 tsp
1 tsp	baking soda	1 tsp
½ cup	walnuts**	50 g

* medium-sized ones, weighing about 4 oz/115 g each, unpeeled
** or Brazil nuts

Since we are in the territory of items to be buttered, we'll begin with a recipe that, although nicely moist and with very good keeping qualities, includes no butter in the mixture. Buttering a slice of this delicious loaf before you eat it is therefore practically obligatory, rather than indulgent. It is very fast and easy to make, but you do need bananas that are very ripe so they mash up well: they are the source of most of the moisture. Like many simple loaf recipes, this one lends itself to alternative versions – I sometimes chop up a few dried apricots, some crystallised ginger and even a couple of squares of dark chocolate and toss them in.

GETTING READY

Preheat the oven to 350°F/180°C. Lightly grease a medium-sized (8 x 4 in/20 x 10 cm) loaf tin and line the bottom with a rectangle of baking paper. Coarsely chop the nuts.

MIXING AND BAKING

1. Mash the bananas, put them into a bowl and break the eggs in on top of them. Beat very well together with a wooden spoon. Stir in the sugar, then sift on the flour, salt and baking soda. Mix everything together, then add the nuts.
2. Spoon the mixture into the prepared tin, smooth the top and bake for about 1 hour, rotating the tin halfway through to ensure the loaf browns evenly.
3. When the loaf is well risen and browned, test it by pressing lightly in the centre with your finger – it should spring back. Remove it from the oven and after about 5 minutes turn it out onto a rack to cool, remove the baking paper and turn it up the right way again. Store airtight, once it is cool.

BANANA NOTE

If you have bananas that are very ripe – perfect for making this loaf or for a banana cake – you can keep them in the freezer until you are ready to start baking. The skins will turn black, but when they defrost they will mash very smoothly. Incidentally, I think the easiest way to do this is to place the whole peeled banana on a dinner plate, hold it steady and work your way along it mashing it thoroughly with a table fork. If you have your own method, use it by all means.

Boston Bun

FOR THE DOUGH

1 cup	mashed potato	1 cup
¾ cup	sugar	150 g
2 cups	flour	250 g
2 tsp	baking powder	2 tsp
¼ tsp	salt	¼ tsp
1 cup	milk	225 ml
1 cup	dried fruit*	140 g

* mostly sultanas and maybe some mixed peel

FOR THE TOPPING

2 oz	butter	55 g
2 cups	icing sugar	240 g
1-2 tbsp	milk	1-2 tbsp
2-3	drops red food colouring	2-3
½ cup	desiccated coconut	40 g

BOSTON BUN NOTE

When I first made this recipe I was a little disappointed that the buns were so shallow, and putting the dough into a deeper tin didn't help since it made the texture too heavy. But Boston Bun remained a favourite with my tasters at Inhouse Design and I was reassured by Jason Mildren's (unsolicited) comment that the shallowness was an advantage, since the problem with bought Boston Buns is that you can't bite into them without getting icing on the end of your nose.

A soft, white, fruity 'tea bread' with a good layer of fluffy icing on top (pink or white) and desiccated coconut pressed into the icing, this is a New Zealand favourite. Although iced, it is perfectly proper to spread it – lavishly – with butter. I found this recipe in the 1981 *Catholic Women's League, Dunedin Diocese Cookbook*, contributed by Dorothy (Dot) Lavelle of Winton, near Invercargill. Her recipe ends, very accurately, with the word 'Delicious!' The mashed potato in the dough makes the bread soft and springy and keeps it fresh for several days. This will make two shallow round loaves: one to eat at home and one to give away – an honourable tradition.

GETTING READY

Preheat the oven to 350°F/180°C and grease and flour two shallow round sponge tins, 8 in/20 cm in diameter. Make sure the potato is cold and lump-free. Push it through a sieve if you need to. Sift the flour, baking powder and salt together.

MIXING AND BAKING

1. Beat the mashed potato and sugar in a bowl until smooth, then add the sifted dry ingredients, the milk and lastly the fruit. Divide the mixture between the prepared tins and smooth the tops with a flat-bladed knife.
2. Bake for 30 minutes, rotating the tins after 20 minutes. When the buns are golden brown and springy to the touch, remove them from the oven, let them rest for a few minutes and then turn them out onto a wire rack. Ice the tops while they are slightly warm – not hot, or the icing will run off.

FINISHING

Cream the butter with the sifted icing sugar and a little warm milk and keep beating until the icing is really soft. Colour it pale pink – or bright pink – if you wish, spread it thickly on the tops of the buns, then press lots of desiccated coconut into it. Serve cut into slices with butter for spreading.

NOTE

Commercial versions of these buns, made with yeast, are called Boston Buns in the South Island and Sally Lunns in the North. None bear any resemblance to an English Sally Lunn or Soleilune Cake, as baked in Bath, which is a yeast bread enriched with egg and cream and glazed with a sweet syrup after baking – but with no sugar in the dough, no sultanas, no icing and certainly no coconut, according to Elizabeth David.† I haven't found the source of the name Boston Bun, but it seems to appear in New Zealand and Australia. In the 1976 edition of the *P.W.M.U.* (Presbyterian Women's Missionary Union) *Cookery Book*, first published in Melbourne in 1904, I found a recipe for a Boston Bun Loaf, made from a very similar mixture, but un-iced.

† **Elizabeth David, *English Bread and Yeast Cookery*, Penguin, 1977, page 467.**

Jocelyn's Cheese Muffins

INGREDIENTS

1½ cups	flour	180 g
4 tsp*	baking powder	3½ tsp
½ tsp	salt	½ tsp
pinch	cayenne pepper	pinch
1 cup	tasty cheese**	80 g
2 tbsp	chopped parsley	2 tbsp
1	egg	1
¾ cup	milk	190 ml
2-3 tbsp	grated Parmesan	2-3 tbsp

* small
** grated

During my years working at the Auckland Art Gallery, the quality of baking at the Art Gallery Café was a major contributor to staff morale. I fondly remember racing up the stairs at 10 in the morning to make sure I didn't miss out on Jocelyn Strewe's warm cheese muffins, and then sitting outside on the balcony with colleagues while everyone polished off one or two of these crunchy-topped golden beauties. Jocelyn kindly gave me her recipe and these are the only muffins I make – apart from the very occasional Bran Muffin. They are right up there with Cheese Scones and just about the perfect savoury accompaniment to a mid-morning coffee.

GETTING READY

Preheat the oven to 400°F/200°C. Grease 12 regular-sized muffin tins. Sift the flour, baking powder, salt and cayenne together. Bring the egg to room temperature.

MIXING AND BAKING

1. Place the dry ingredients in a large bowl and add half the cheese and the parsley. Mix everything together with a table knife. Beat the egg and milk together, pour into the dry ingredients and mix until everything is just combined. Don't overmix.
2. Spoon into the muffin tins and top with the remaining grated cheese and a good sprinkling of parmesan.
3. Bake for 10–15 minutes until golden brown and smelling cooked. Turn out onto a rack to cool and serve as soon as possible.

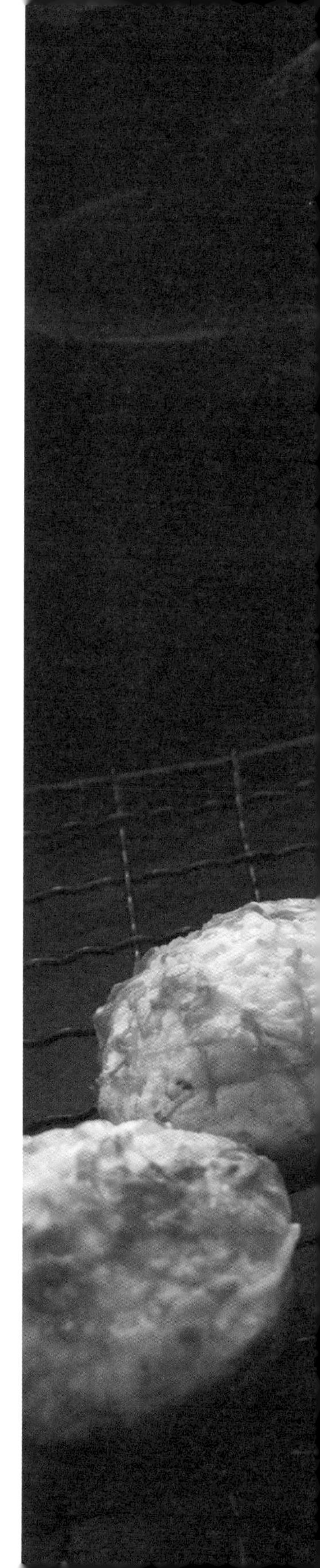

Laughing Jennies

INGREDIENTS

8 oz	**flour**	**225 g**
½ tsp	**baking powder**	**½ tsp**
4 oz	**butter**	**115 g**
½ cup	**currants**	**70 g**
3 tbsp	**water**	**45 ml**
	extra sugar, for sprinkling	

A name that's very hard to resist and a biscuit to match. These are small, square currant biscuits with no sweetening in the mixture – just a sprinkling of granulated sugar on top for crunch. And you serve them buttered, of course. The recipe was contributed by D. Bennett to *Our Recipe Book*, published in 1967 by the Karitane Public Hall Building Committee. The next recipe on the page is for Laughing Jinnies; similar, but with sugar and sultanas in the mix. I prefer the sugar on the outside.

GETTING READY

Preheat the oven to 425°F/215°C and lightly grease an oven tray, or line it with baking paper.

MIXING AND BAKING

1. Sift the flour and baking powder into a large mixing bowl and drop in the butter, cut into smallish cubes. Rub the butter into the flour using your fingertips, or a pastry blender, or you could use a food processor. You don't need the mixture to be too finely blended – tiny lumps of butter will make the biscuits more flaky. Add the currants and mix everything to a firm dough with cold water. You will probably need about 3 tablespoons, but add the water gradually. If the dough gets too wet and sticky it will be hard to handle.
2. Turn the dough onto a floured board and roll out as thinly as you can. Roll from the centre to the edge with firm strokes and rotate the dough as you go, keeping it moving on the board and sprinkling more flour underneath if you need to. You can work with half the dough at a time if that seems easier.
3. Now cut the dough into squares – the size is up to you, but I make them about 2½ in/6 cm square. Transfer them carefully to your baking sheet, leaving just a small gap between them – they won't spread very much. Brush them lightly with cold water using a pastry brush and sprinkle with sugar. Bake for about 10 minutes until they are just golden, rotating the tray halfway through. Store airtight and serve buttered. Makes about 24.

Our Recipe Book, compiled by the Karitane Public Hall Building Committee in 1967. The first chapter opens with this maxim: 'No mean cook can cook well; it calls for a generous spirit, a light hand, and a large heart.'

Pikelets Supreme

INGREDIENTS

2	eggs	2
½ cup	brown sugar	100 g
¾ cup	milk	170 ml
1½ cups	flour	180 g
pinch*	salt	⅛ tsp
1 tsp	baking soda	1 tsp
1 tsp**	cream of tartar	1½ tsp
1 dsp	melted butter	20 ml

* a good pinch
** heaped tsp

Pikelets Supreme were contributed by 'W.F.I., Texas' to the *Khandallah Cookery Book*, compiled by Khandallah Presbyterian Church in Wellington and published in 1950. I imagined an expatriate New Zealander adapting pikelets for American tastes, but Jenny Orange revealed W.F.I. to be Willi Inder – a petite and vivacious Texan redhead with a lovely accent, who married New Zealand engineer Rex Inder and came to live in Wellington. The brown sugar gives her pikelets a slightly caramel flavour and makes them sweeter than the Perfect Pikelets in *Ladies, a Plate*. But they are every bit as delicious.

GETTING READY

Put a heavy-based frying pan or a cast iron griddle on a medium element to heat up. You want to bring it gently up to heat, not have it blazing hot. (You are mimicking the gentle, even heat on the top of a coal range.) Put a folded clean tea towel onto a board beside the stove. As you make the pikelets you'll cover them with the tea towel to keep them warm and soft. Sift together the flour, salt, baking soda and cream of tartar.

MIXING AND COOKING

1. Put the eggs and brown sugar into a mixing bowl and beat with a rotary beater or a whisk until pale and fluffy. This will take about a minute. Tip in the milk, then the dry ingredients and lastly the melted butter. Mix quickly to the consistency of thick cream.
2. Grease the surface of your pan very lightly with butter. Use a tablespoon or a dessertspoon to drop the batter onto the griddle – hold the spoon vertically and pour from the tip and the circles will be perfect. Make about four at a time. When bubbles appear on the top of the pikelets and begin to burst, flip them over carefully with a thin spatula and cook the other side for about 30 seconds until lightly browned. Pile your pikelets between two layers of the clean tea towel and keep going until they are all cooked. Serve hot with butter and honey or home-made jam. Makes about 24 pikelets.

Puftaloons

INGREDIENTS

½ lb	flour	225 g
1½ tsp	baking powder	1½ tsp
pinch	salt	pinch
¾ cup	milk	170 ml
	oil for deep frying	
	icing sugar, for dusting	

NOTE

'Singing Hinnies' from Northumberland are cooked on the griddle, not fried. They are made from a sweet and buttery scone dough leavened with baking powder, mixed with cream and buttermilk, and studded with sultanas or currants. Like Chris's fried scones, they 'sing' when they are ready to be turned. In the famous *Green and Gold Cookery Book*, published by King's College, Adelaide, in 1923 and still in print, Fried Scones are pronounced 'useful when short of bread and a substitute needed in a hurry… They are nice fried in bacon fat and served with bacon, but are delicious if fried in lard or good dripping, drained well and eaten with honey or maple syrup and butter.' I should probably mention that digestibility is not one of the virtues of these little rascals.

This intriguing word seems to have been applied to a variety of dishes, but here it means plain scones, made with no butter and fried rather than baked in the oven or on the griddle. They puff up as they cook and are really a sort of doughnut made with baking powder rather than yeast. Beth, of Henderson, whose recipe for them was published in Aunt Daisy's 1934 *Cookery Book*, cut the centres out with a thimble to give them the characteristic doughnut hole. They are not part of my childhood memories, but a friend, Chris Szekely, told me he regularly made them as a treat for his sister and himself when they arrived home hungry after school. In his South Auckland family they were known as 'Singing Ninnies', because you rolled them over when they 'sang' or sizzled. Chris drained them on crumpled brown paper, sprinkled them with icing sugar, and everyone ate them hot, filled with butter and jam, or golden syrup.

GETTING READY

Gently heat some oil, fat or lard in a frying pan, 1–2 in/2.5–5 cm deep, until it is very hot. Tiny bubbles should form against the side of a wooden spoon when you dip it into the oil.

MIXING AND FRYING

1. Sift the dry ingredients together, pour in the milk and mix to a light dough with a table knife. Turn out onto a floured board, knead lightly and roll out to ½ in/1.5 cm thick.
2. Cut into squares for easy splitting and buttering – or rounds, in which case you can remove the centres with a thimble or a small round cutter.
3. Place them gently in the hot oil. (The little round centres should be cooked too, of course, if you can extricate them from the thimble.) Turn them over when they 'sing' and remove when they are golden brown and puffed. Drain on brown paper or paper towels, dredge with icing sugar, and serve hot.

Marmalade Tea Loaf

INGREDIENTS

4 oz	**sultanas**	**115 g**
4 oz	**currants**	**115 g**
4 oz	**sugar**	**115 g**
4 oz	**marmalade**	**115 g**
1 cup	**hot tea**	**225 ml**
1	**egg**	**1**
8 oz	**flour**	**225 g**
2 tsp	**baking powder**	**2 tsp**

I found this fruity Tea Loaf in *Recipes Old and New*, compiled and published by the Moana Rua Ladies and Brighton Life Saving Clubs, probably in the early 1970s. The currants and sultanas are soaked in tea overnight, as is usual with these recipes, but with the surprising addition of some marmalade, which contributes a lovely sharp flavour. You can use bought marmalade, but if you have made your own – see recipe on page 124 – here is the perfect way to bring top-quality marmalade further into your day. Why limit it to breakfast time? Although a slice of this loaf would make a very fine breakfast indeed.

Recipes, Old & New, compiled and published by Moana Rua Ladies and Brighton Life Saving Clubs, includes a useful guide for ordering vegetables, fruit and meat to feed 25 people and a page of safety directions for Surf Bathers. These include, of course: 'Don't bathe directly after a meal.'

GETTING READY

The night before you want to bake the loaf, put the sultanas, currants, sugar and marmalade in a large bowl (I chop the peel in the marmalade if it is in long shreds) and pour the hot tea over – any variety of tea will do. Cover the bowl with a plate or cloth and leave on the bench overnight. The next day preheat the oven to 325°F/160°C. Grease and flour your baking tin very thoroughly. You can use a 10 x 4½ in/25 x 11 cm loaf tin, in which case put a piece of baking paper in the base of the tin before flouring it, or a nut roll tin as I did. I like the look of the circular slices, but the recipe makes 3½ cups of mixture, which was too much for my nut roll tin, so I baked the extra as a mini-loaf. Bring the egg to room temperature and sift together the flour and baking powder.

MIXING AND BAKING

1. Add the unbeaten egg to the soaked fruit and beat well with a wooden spoon. Gently mix in the sifted dry ingredients.
2. Scoop the mixture into the tin or tins and bake for about 75 minutes. Roll tins should be placed upright on a baking tray or other shallow tin and so must be on a low rack in the oven.
3. Remove the tins from the oven and put on a rack to cool. Don't try to remove the loaf from a roll tin for at least 10 minutes or it may break. Store airtight and serve sliced and buttered.

WHICH TIN TO USE?

Cooks do not always have a wide variety of cake tins to choose from, so ingenuity is called for in the search for substitutes. In Elsie Harvey's copy of the 1940s *Dunedin City Gas Department Cookery Book*, lent to me by her grandson Dean Parker, I came across the comment that a Nut and Raisin Loaf recipe was 'Sufficient to fill 3 Baking Powder tins'. And a few pages earlier was a recipe for 'Small Meat Pies, which may be cooked in Tobacco Tins'. You may not be reduced to tobacco tins, but you could use any empty tins for this sort of plain loaf as long as they are not more than two-thirds full of mixture and are well greased and floured. A good plan is to measure the capacity of your tins in cups of water and put the loaf mixture into a glass measuring cup to see how much you have. And make a note beside the recipe so you'll know next time if the substitution was a success.

Welsh Cakes

INGREDIENTS

6 oz	butter*	170 g
1 lb	self-raising flour	450 g
6 oz	caster sugar	170 g
1 tsp	baking powder	1 tsp
½ tsp	mixed spice	½ tsp
3 oz	currants	75 g
2	eggs	2
	extra caster sugar, for dusting	

* or lard and butter mixed

NOTE

Dorothy Fitzgerald sent Bryony Dalefield a copy of *Ladies, a Plate* and Bryony responded by making two 'ceremonial pot mits', one for Dorothy and one for me. Bryony's ability to design and stitch such a beautiful object is breathtaking and her generous gift brings me daily delight. I don't use it, I just look at it, touch it – and marvel.

Some New Zealand recipe books call these Welsh Tea Cakes or Welsh Cake Johnnies, but they are not as familiar as pikelets, which they resemble. I first tasted Welsh Cakes when a friend, Bryony Dalefield, bought some for me at the Women's Institutes stall in Chepstow in Wales where she lives. This recipe comes from a cookbook Bryony has, called *Lamb, Leeks and Laver Bread: The Best of Welsh Cookery*, by Gilli Davies.† Small and tender cakes with a few currants and a dash of spice and cooked on the griddle, they taste very good, they keep very well, they are easily made and – partly because of their unfamiliarity here – they invariably earn an interested and delighted response

GETTING READY

Put a heavy-based frying pan or a cast iron griddle on a medium element to heat up. You want to bring it gently up to heat and not have it blazing hot. (You are mimicking the gentle, even heat on the top of a coal range.) Put a folded clean tea towel onto a board beside the stove. As you make the Welsh Cakes you'll cover them with the tea towel to keep them warm and soft. Beat the eggs.

MIXING AND COOKING

1. Rub the fat into the flour, then mix in the dry ingredients. Add the currants, then pour in the beaten eggs and mix to a firm dough. You will probably have to knead it by hand at the end. Add a tablespoon of milk if the dough won't come together.
2. Working with a quarter or half the dough at a time, on a lightly floured board roll out the dough and stamp into 2 in/5 cm circles using a cutter – fluted or not as you wish. I make them about a ¼ in/7 mm thick.
3. Cook very gently for 3–4 minutes on each side. They burn easily, so keep the heat low. They will puff up nicely as they cook.
4. Put them between the folds of the tea towel, dusting them with caster sugar as you go. Dust with more caster sugar and eat immediately – by themselves, or with butter and/or jam. Store airtight. They freeze well.

I often make a half recipe as the full amount makes several dozen Welsh Cakes, almost enough for an Eisteddfod.

† Davies, Gilli, *Lamb, Leeks and Laver Bread: The Best of Welsh Cookery*, Grafton, London, 1989.

DEAR ALEXA
THANK
for the recipes

Festive
Baking

Any of the baking in this chapter would make a very acceptable gift, whether you are looking for something plainly and simply delicious, or a more decorative, rich and celebratory offering. Dried fruit, nuts and spices have long been associated with feasting at special times of the year and even in New Zealand, where Christmas is a summer festival, small tarts made from a buttery shortcrust and filled with home-made fruit mincemeat are very hard to resist. At Easter time a golden currant biscuit can symbolise a farewell to the sun as winter approaches, rather than a welcome to its return in spring, and Simnel Cake is an essential annual treat no matter where you live.

You could make a gingery Yorkshire Parkin any time of the year, but do have some ready for 5 November – the night when Yorkshire remembers one of its most infamous sons, Guy Fawkes, and Parkin is eaten beside the bonfires. And as the end of the year approaches, try to set aside a morning to make Spicy Speculaas biscuits or Swedish Coffee Bread and enjoy the wonderful spicy aromas, the pleasant processes of baking and the delighted responses of your family and friends.

Brazil Nut Fingers

FOR THE BASE

4 oz	**butter**	**125 g**
½ cup	**sugar**	**100 g**
2	**eggs**	**2**
1 cup	**flour**	**125 g**
1 tsp	**baking powder**	**1 tsp**
½ cup	**Brazil nuts**	**70 g**

FOR THE TOPPING

2 oz	**butter**	**55 g**
¾ cup	**brown sugar**	**150 g**
1 tsp	**mixed spice**	**1 tsp**

FOR THE ICING

1 tbsp	**lemon juice**	**1 tbsp**
1 cup	**icing sugar**	**120 g**

In New Zealand we still associate nuts with Christmas – one of many customs lingering from the northern hemisphere's mid-winter celebration. These pretty fingers, with their spicy, buttery topping, spongy base and delicious chopped Brazils, are festive in appearance, easy to make and extremely edible. My version is written on an index card, unsourced but no doubt copied from a magazine, and I found a very similar recipe contributed by Dawn Bennett to *St Columba's Presbyterian Church, Havelock North, Recipe Book* – probably from the mid-1970s. Whatever the source, they are well worth making today.

GETTING READY

Preheat the oven to 375°F/190°C and line a shallow 12 x 8 in/ 30 x 21 cm tin with baking paper, or grease it lightly. Bring the butter to room temperature, and chop Brazil nuts into rough thirds or halves – the pieces should be quite large. Sift together the flour and baking powder.

MIXING AND BAKING

1. Cream the butter and sugar until pale and fluffy, then beat in the eggs and the dry ingredients. Spread evenly in the prepared tin and distribute the chopped nuts over the top.
2. Melt the butter in a small saucepan and mix in the brown sugar and spice. Use a teaspoon to dollop the topping over the nuts – you won't be able to spread it, but make sure the surface is fairly evenly dotted with the spicy mix.
3. Bake for 20 minutes, rotating the tin halfway through. When cooked, the base should be golden brown, with the cake mixture puffed up around the nuts and the spicy topping. Allow to cool on a wire rack.

FINISHING

Mix enough lemon juice into the icing sugar to make a fairly runny icing. Put the icing into a small paper piping bag (see page 10 for instructions on how to make one) or a small plastic bag. Cut off the point of the piping bag or one corner of the plastic bag and drizzle the icing in free-form festive squiggles over the bumpy surface of the cake. Cut into squares or fingers once the icing has set. Store airtight. Makes 24.

Easter Biscuits

INGREDIENTS

5 oz	butter	140 g
4 oz	caster sugar	115 g
1 tsp	lemon zest	1 tsp
2	egg yolks	2
8 oz	flour	225 g
¼ cup	currants	35 g
pinch	mixed spice*	pinch

* or cinnamon

GLAZE

1	egg white	1
	caster sugar, extra	

NOTE
These are the iced biscuits that appear on the cover of this book. I left out the currants and used a fancy biscuit cutter. You could sprinkle them with coloured sugar before you bake them or decorate them as I did with royal icing, made from an egg white mixed with 1½ cups/180 g icing sugar.

Crisp, lemony, sugary and golden, these currant biscuits are an English recipe that appears in a number of early New Zealand cookery books – one of the many festival foods that migrated to the Antipodes with British settlers. In the West Country their colour and shape and their rich ingredients celebrate the end of Lenten fasting and the coming of spring. They are simply made and they don't look dramatic, but they do taste wonderful. Make them for afternoon tea on Easter Sunday.

GETTING READY
Preheat the oven to 375°F/190°C and line an oven tray with a sheet of baking paper. Bring the butter to room temperature. Finely grate the zest of the lemon.

MIXING AND BAKING

1. Cream the butter and sugar with the lemon rind, add the egg yolks and mix well. Work in the flour, spice and the currants until you have a fairly stiff paste. Put the dough in the fridge in a bowl, covered, and leave it to firm up for 10–15 minutes.
2. Sprinkle the bench with cornflour or rice flour to help stop the dough from sticking, and roll it out fairly thinly. Use a large fluted cutter (about 3 in/ 8 cm in diameter) to cut circles, and place them on the baking paper. Brush with lightly beaten egg white – just whisk it enough to make it liquid – and sprinkle them with caster sugar.
3. Bake for 10–15 minutes, rotating the tray after 5 minutes. Easter Biscuits should be a light golden colour. Store airtight. Makes about 24.

Christmas Mincemeat and Mince Pies

FOR THE MINCEMEAT

1 lb	suet or butter	450 g
2 lb	apples	900 g
1½ lb	raisins	675 g
1 lb	currants	450 g
1 lb	sultanas	450 g
8 oz	mixed peel	225 g
4 oz	ground almonds	115 g
1 lb	sugar	450 g
1 oz	mixed spice	2 tbsp
¼ tsp	ground nutmeg	¼ tsp
4	lemons*	4
	brandy**	300 ml

* grated zest and juice
** 2 wine glasses

FOR THE PASTRY

3 cups	flour	375 g
½ cup	icing sugar	60 g
pinch	salt	pinch
½ lb	butter	225 g
1	egg, beaten	1
2 tbsp	milk	2 tbsp
	caster sugar, for dusting	

PASTRY NOTE

This short pastry is easy to make and to handle and is absolutely perfect for Christmas Mince Pies. (It also works if you use half caster and half icing sugar.) The recipe came from Betty Shaw of Taumarunui, who called it Ella's Pastry since it was from her friend Ella Steadman.

This is Elizabeth Messenger's 1957 recipe for Christmas Mincemeat which she headed 'Make it early', since it needs to be stored for a month before using. The mixture makes eight 1lb (400 ml) jars, which will keep almost indefinitely, and the flavour and texture are my idea of perfection.

MAKING THE MINCEMEAT

1. Have the suet or butter at room temperature. Peel and quarter the apples and mince them with the dried fruit, or pulse them in the food processor. This is essential since you don't want lumps of unchopped fruit – everything should be amalgamated, not to a sludge but to a slightly lumpy paste. Put the mixture in a large bowl.
2. Add the almonds, suet or butter, sugar and spices and mix well with your hands, then add the lemon zest and juice and the brandy. Stir thoroughly and store in well-washed jars with good lids. Store for a month before using. Keeps for 1–2 years.

MAKING THE PASTRY

1. Sift together the flour, icing sugar and salt, then rub in the butter until the mixture looks like coarse breadcrumbs.
2. Add the egg a little at a time and knead lightly to form a smooth paste (this can be done in the food processor). Use the milk if you need to. Wrap in paper and refrigerate for at least an hour before using.

MAKING THE MINCE PIES

1. Preheat the oven to 430°F/220°C. Roll out the pastry on a floured board to a thickness of 1⁄16 in/2 mm and cut out 24 rounds of the same size. Line 12 patty tins with rounds of pastry, brush the edges with water, fill with a generous spoonful of mincemeat, mounding it up, and top each with another round of pastry. Fit the top inside the lower round and push the edges together gently. Make a small hole in the centre of each top with a skewer.
2. Bake for about 20 minutes, rotating the trays after 10 minutes. Remove from the oven when they are golden brown and place the tins on a rack. Sprinkle the tops with caster sugar and serve warm if you can. Makes 24.

In his wonderful book *First Catch Your Weka: A Story of New Zealand Cooking*,* David Veart applauds the achievements of Elizabeth Messenger (1908–1965), who began writing her 'Dine with Elizabeth' columns in Wellington's *Evening Post* newspaper in 1948 and continued for 15 years. Three books of her collected columns were published in 1956, 1957 and 1961. They stayed in print for a decade and my copies are well thumbed and very well used since, as David Veart noted, Elizabeth Messenger was a lively, intelligent writer, in tune with the needs of her readers and a very good cook.

* **David Veart, *First Catch Your Weka: A Story of New Zealand Cooking*, Auckland University Press, 2008.**

Petticoat Tails, for Tea

INGREDIENTS

6 oz	**flour**	**180 g**
1½ oz	**rice flour**	**45 g**
2 oz	**caster sugar**	**55 g**
pinch	**baking powder**	**pinch**
pinch	**salt**	**pinch**
5 oz	**butter**	**140 g**
	caster sugar, for dusting	

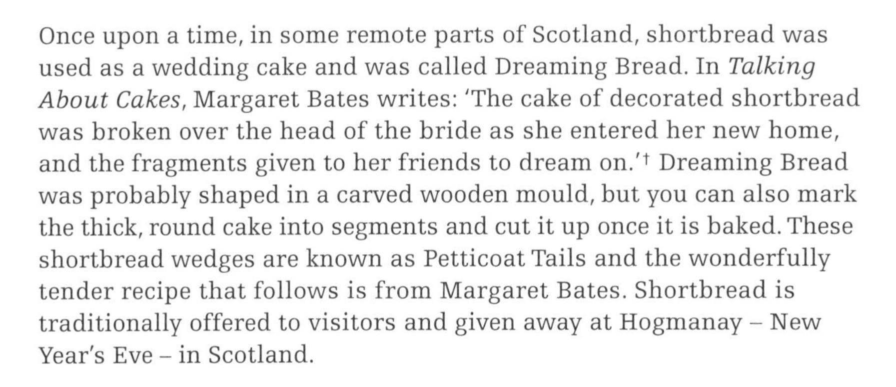
Once upon a time, in some remote parts of Scotland, shortbread was used as a wedding cake and was called Dreaming Bread. In *Talking About Cakes*, Margaret Bates writes: 'The cake of decorated shortbread was broken over the head of the bride as she entered her new home, and the fragments given to her friends to dream on.'† Dreaming Bread was probably shaped in a carved wooden mould, but you can also mark the thick, round cake into segments and cut it up once it is baked. These shortbread wedges are known as Petticoat Tails and the wonderfully tender recipe that follows is from Margaret Bates. Shortbread is traditionally offered to visitors and given away at Hogmanay – New Year's Eve – in Scotland.

GETTING READY

Preheat the oven to 300°F/150°C and line a baking tray with baking paper, or grease it lightly. Bring the butter to room temperature, or you can leave it cold if you are using a food processor. Draw a pencil circle about 7 in/18 cm in diameter on the back of a piece of waxed paper.

MIXING, SHAPING AND BAKING

1. Sift the flours into a bowl, add the sugar and butter, and gradually knead everything until firm – or pulse everything in a food processor until it forms small clumps. Tip out and knead until smooth.
2. Flatten the dough with your hand, put it in the centre of the pencil circle, cover with another piece of waxed paper and roll it out to a circle, trying to keep a good shape. It should be about ½ in/12 mm thick. Remove the top layer of waxed paper, slip your hand carefully underneath the other piece and flip the shortbread onto the baking paper on the tray. This ensures you get the best surface on the top.
3. Make indentations all around the outside with a table fork or pinch it into a frilly rim by pushing the edge with the thumb and forefinger of one hand and the forefinger of the other. Take a long knife and mark the shortbread into 8 segments, then prickle it with the dabber of your choice – a table fork is fine – and put it in the fridge to chill for about 20 minutes. This chilling firms the butter, helps the shortbread keep its shape and is essential if you have used a carved wooden mould to shape your shortbread.

4. Bake it for about 1 hour, rotating the tray halfway through. The shortbread should be a very pale golden colour and smell buttery and cooked. Remove the tray from the oven, slide the baking paper and shortbread onto a wooden board and cut it carefully into segments along the knife-lines you have made. Slide it onto a cooling rack and sprinkle lightly with caster sugar for sparkle. Store airtight when cold.

† **Bates, Margaret, *Talking About Cakes, with an Irish and Scottish Accent*, Pergamon Press, Oxford, 1964, page 104.**

Here is a description of making Petticoat Tails from the oldest cookery book I have, given to me by Peter Wells. Published in Edinburgh in 1804, it is called *The Practice of Cookery, Pastry and Confectionary* (sic) and its author was Mrs Frazer, 'Teacher of these arts in Edinburgh'. Mrs Frazer's enormous recipe begins with three pounds of butter, includes caraway seeds and is headed 'Petticoat Tails, for Tea'. After dividing the mixture into six parts and rolling each into a circle, she continues: 'Prickle it with a dabber. Turn over a flat dinner plate, and cut the bread round by it with a paste runner. Then take off the plate, lay on a saucer, and cut it the same size. Keep the middle circle whole, and divide the other into eight quarters with the runner. Roll out the other parts in like manner, and fire them nicely.'‡ I couldn't resist Mrs Frazer's 'prickling with a dabber', so for this smaller version of Petticoat Tails I use a South Indian bread pricker given to me by Diane McKinnon, a well-travelled friend – and a marvellous cook.

‡ **Mrs Frazer, *The Practice of Cookery, Pastry and Confectionary*, Peter Hill, Edinburgh, 1804, page 210.**

Simnel Cake

FOR THE CAKE

6 oz	butter	170 g
6 oz	caster sugar	170 g
4	eggs	4
6 oz	flour	170 g
8 oz	sultanas	225 g
8 oz	raisins	225 g
2 oz	candied peel	55 g
2 tsp	mixed spice	2 tsp
½ tsp	baking powder	½ tsp

FOR THE ALMOND PASTE IN THE CENTRE

6 oz	ground almonds	170 g
3 oz	caster sugar	85 g
3 oz	icing sugar	85 g
2 drops	almond essence*	2 drops
1	egg	1
	a handful of blanched almonds (optional)	

* or replace with 1 tsp rosewater or orange-flower water

Margaret Bates, Talking About Cakes, with an Irish and Scottish Accent, Pergamon Press, Oxford, 1964. Miss Bates notes, 'The adjective "home-made" is one which rings of the highest praise when used in connection with cakes.'

An utterly delicious idea – to bake a round of almond paste in the middle of a light fruit cake so it becomes an almost fudge-like marzipan layer. To be completely traditional you can then top the cake with more almond paste and a decorative finish of your choosing. Simnel Cake seems originally to have been a treat for Mothering Sunday in the middle of Lent when there was a break in the 40 days of fasting leading up to Good Friday. Today it is associated with Easter Sunday feasting. Margaret Bates describes her recipe as 'a good cutting cake… luscious, spicy, rich and good to eat'. It is my favourite. Miss Bates also notes very wisely: 'When setting out to mix a Simnel Cake try to have plenty of time for the work in hand… two mixtures must be prepared, before it can be put in the oven and so leisure is necessary if one is to enjoy making the cake.'†

GETTING READY

Line an 8 in/23 cm cake tin with baking paper and preheat the oven to 325°F/160°C. Bring the butter to room temperature. Make the almond paste by combining all the ingredients except the egg in a bowl or a food processor, then add just enough beaten egg to make a firm paste. Roll out the paste between two sheets of waxed paper to the size of your cake tin. It should be about ½ in/1.5 cm thick. Set aside.

MIXING AND BAKING

1. Cream the butter and sugar until light and fluffy. Add the beaten eggs alternately with the flour and lastly stir in the fruit, spice and baking powder.
2. Put half the mixture into the lined cake tin. (I weigh the whole mix, then halve it to make sure I get the proportions right, but this isn't strictly necessary.) Place the almond paste on top, press it gently into position and then add the remaining cake mixture. Level the top with a damp hand to stop fruit from poking out and burning. If you intend adding a top layer of almond paste later, leave the cake plain; otherwise a few rows of blanched almonds arranged around the top look suitably festive.
3. Bake for about 2½ hours until golden and firm to the touch and shrinking a little from the sides of the tin. (Testing with a skewer is difficult because of the almond paste, which remains sticky.) Leave to cool in the tin, then turn out and remove the baking paper.

FINISHING

You can serve the cake as it is – with or without the whole almonds on top – and no one will complain, but if you want to be more traditional you can do the following: Make another batch of almond paste using 8 oz/225 g almonds and 4 oz/115 g each of caster and sifted icing sugar, and beaten egg to mix. Roll two-thirds of it out between layers of waxed paper, roughly to the size of the tin. Brush the paste lightly with beaten egg and invert the cake onto it. Press well together and trim away any excess paste with a sharp knife. Turn the cake over and decorate with the remaining almond paste – 11 balls of paste are said to represent the 11 faithful apostles. Finally brown the top very quickly under a hot grill.

NOTE

Here is a suggestion for decorating your cake from Miss Bates:

'First of all a pleasant effect may be obtained by pressing the almond paste with a wire cake cooler. You will find this marks it neatly into little squares. Then pinch around the edge as you would a round of shortbread and decorate with balls of almond paste, stuck into place with egg… Brush the balls with more egg and toast a pretty golden colour in a hot oven. The almond paste should brown in under 5 minutes if the temperature is correct. The centre now remains to be decorated and here the artist has great opportunity. A favourite method of mine is to pile neatly cut glace fruits in the centre of the cake. Suggested fruit would include a mixture of cherries, pineapple and angelica… In order to hold them in position, a little water icing should be spread over the centre part of the cake and, while it is still moist, the fruit is piled on top in such a way as to completely hide the icing.[‡]

[†,‡] Bates, Margaret, *Talking About Cakes, with an Irish and Scottish Accent*, Pergamon Press, Oxford, 1964, page 167.

Spicy Speculaas

FOR THE DOUGH

10 oz	butter	280 g
1 lb 2 oz	flour	560 g
4 tsp	speculaas spices*	4 tsp
2 tsp	baking powder	2 tsp
¼ tsp	salt	¼ tsp
8 oz	caster sugar	225 g
2 tsp	lemon zest**	2 tsp
1	egg, beaten	1

* See note on page 115 or use mixed spice.
** finely grated

FOR THE ALMOND PASTE FILLING

6 oz	ground almonds	170 g
3 oz	caster sugar	85 g
3 oz	icing sugar	85 g
2 drops	almond essence†	2 drops
1	egg, beaten	1

† or 1 tsp rosewater or orange-flower water

TO FINISH

1	egg, beaten	1
80	blanched almonds	80

Speculaas are traditional Dutch biscuits made in quantity for Sinterklaas – the feast of St Nicholas, which is celebrated on 6 December. St Nicholas was Bishop of Myra in Turkey in the fourth century and known for his affection for children, his protection of the defenceless and for his mysterious, generous giving. Dutch settlers in North America brought with them the tradition of leaving gifts for children by the fireplace on 5 December, the eve of his feast day, and so created the modern figure of Santa Claus. The delicious dough was pressed into decorative carved wooden moulds – some old ones had an image of Sinterklaas with his long beard and sack of presents – or made into little balls, flattened down and topped with a blanched almond, or best of all, I think, rolled out and filled with almond paste. They all taste good and are the perfect thing to have in the tin for Christmas visitors, as their spicy flavour keeps improving for several weeks.

GETTING READY

Make the almond paste by combining the almonds, sugar and flavouring and mix to a firm paste with the egg. Knead until smooth, wrap in waxed paper and set aside. Bring the butter and egg to room temperature. Sift together the flour, spices, baking powder and salt.

MIXING THE DOUGH

1. Cut the butter into small lumps and rub it into the dry ingredients with your fingertips until the mixture resembles breadcrumbs. This can be done in a food processor.
2. Mix in the sugar and lemon zest, then add enough of the egg to make a firm paste. Knead well, divide into two rectangular blocks, wrap in waxed paper and set aside in a cool place – not the fridge – for a couple of hours.

SHAPING AND BAKING

1. Preheat the oven to 340°F/170°C. Flour a piece of baking paper and roll out one-half of the dough directly onto the paper. Aim to have a rectangle about 14 x 10 in/35 x 25 cm and ⅛ in/3 mm thick.
2. Roll out the almond paste to the same size (it will be only about 1⁄16 in/2 mm thick). Place it carefully on the dough. Don't worry if it breaks or cracks – just patch it with another piece of paste.
3. Roll out the second piece of dough to the same size on another piece of baking paper and invert it carefully onto the almond paste.

(This is tricky, but possible, I assure you. I use a baking sheet to lift the dough, still on its paper, and flip it carefully onto the paste.) Remove the paper and roll lightly over the surface with your floured rolling pin.

4. Brush the surface with beaten egg, arrange the almonds in rows and mark the surface into squares or diamond shapes with the back of a knife, with an almond in the centre of each. Brush again with egg and bake for 30–35 minutes until golden brown, rotating the tray after 20 minutes. Cool on a rack and cut along the marked lines using a long knife. Stored airtight, they keep very well indeed. Makes 80.

SPECULAAS SPICES

You can buy spice mixtures specially blended for Speculaas biscuits at shops selling Dutch groceries, or you could make up a mixture yourself. This is the one I use.

3 oz	**cinnamon**	**6 tbsp**
1 oz	**ground nutmeg**	**2 tbsp**
1 oz	**ground cloves**	**2 tbsp**
1 oz	**ground ginger**	**2 tbsp**
½ oz	**ground aniseed‡**	**1 tbsp**
¼ oz	**ground white pepper**	**1½ tsp**

‡ or ground cardamom

I use ready-ground cinnamon, cloves, ginger and pepper, but I grind the aniseed and nutmeg in a spice grinder so that they are really fresh and aromatic. Blend everything together, sift out any gritty bits and store airtight. This makes a lot, but it keeps well and you could always give some away to a friend – with a batch of your delicious Speculaas and this recipe, of course.

Swedish Coffee Bread

FOR THE DOUGH

1 cup	**warm water**	**225 ml**
4½ tsp	**dried yeast**	**4½ tsp**
½ cup	**butter**	**115 g**
3	**eggs**	**3**
½ cup	**sugar**	**100 g**
1 tsp	**salt**	**1 tsp**
1 tsp	**cardamom***	**1 tsp**
4 cups	**flour**	**500 g**

* ground

FOR THE FILLING

½ cup	**butter**	**115 g**
½ cup	**sugar**	**100 g**
3 tsp	**cinnamon****	**3 tsp**
1 cup	**blanched almonds (optional)**	**100 g**

** or 2 tsp speculaas spice, 1 tsp cinnamon

FOR THE GLAZE

1 cup	**icing sugar**	**120 g**
½ tsp	**almond essence**	**½ tsp**
2 tbsp	**hot coffee†**	**2 tbsp**
	a handful of toasted, flaked almonds	

† or milk

This is my favourite Christmas gift: spectacular to look at, easy to make and delicious to eat. The idea is simple. Roll out a cardamom-scented sweet bread dough, spread it with butter, sprinkle sugar and cinnamon over the top and then roll it up, form into a ring and cut through at intervals with scissors to reveal the spicy, buttery spiral inside. (Saxbröd or Scissor Bread is an alternative name for it.) Many early New Zealand cookery books have recipes for this treat made with scone dough and it relates to the Pinwheel Scones I remember making at intermediate school in the 1960s. But this version is made with a light dough that rises overnight in the fridge and is rolled out while chilled so it is easy to handle. There are many recipes for this in Swedish and Scandinavian cookery books; this version is based on Swedish Coffee Bread in *The Great Scandinavian Baking Book*‡, by Finnish-American Beatrice Ojakangas. Her dough is richer than many and she has streamlined the method of making it, so even though the recipe looks long, the processes are quite simple. It invariably elicits delighted reactions and I think Swedish Coffee Bread should be in every home baker's repertoire.

MIXING

Put the warm water in a large mixing bowl, sprinkle the yeast over and leave to stand for about 5 minutes. Melt the butter and mix it with the beaten eggs, sugar, salt and cardamom. Pour this on top of the yeast and stir, then tip in the flour and mix everything together to form a smooth dough. It will be quite soft, but chilling will firm it up. Transfer to a clean, greased bowl, cover with a plate and put in the fridge for 2–24 hours. I always leave it overnight.

SHAPING

1. Soften the butter for the filling to a good spreading consistency. Preheat the oven to 400°F/200°C and line a large baking tray with baking paper, or grease it lightly. If you have a pizza stone or some quarry tiles, put them in the oven to heat up too. The bread will bake better with a strong heat on the base.
2. Now turn the chilled dough out onto a floured board, large enough for you to roll out a rectangle about 20 x 24 in/50 x 60 cm. Knead the dough lightly, shape it into a rough rectangle and start rolling it out from the centre to the edges, keeping it moving on the board and shaking more flour underneath if necessary. If the dough seems reluctant to stretch and keeps pulling back, cover it with a cloth and

leave it to rest for a few minutes. Practice makes perfect and if you can't extend the dough out to the full size, it doesn't really matter.

3. Once you've done your best with the rolling out, spread the softened butter as evenly as you can over the whole surface (I have sometimes used melted butter and this works fine) and sprinkle thickly with the sugar and spice, and the chopped almonds if you are using them. Roll up the whole thing fairly tightly from one of the longer edges. Seal the final edge by pinching the dough and make sure the seam is underneath the roll. Run your hands along it to even out the thickness, then lift the whole thing onto your prepared baking sheet – tricky, but achievable.
4. Curve the log into a circle, cut about 4 cm off each end and pinch the cut ends together at the base of the circle. (Bake the offcuts as little cinnamon rolls in a separate greased tin – a cook's treat for later.) Take a pair of sharp scissors and work your way around the ring, cutting firmly through the dough, almost to the bottom, at about 2 cm intervals. As you go, twist each disc of dough alternately in and out of the circle, revealing the spiral within. Set aside under a cloth for about 45 minutes, or until puffy.

BAKING

Turn the oven temperature down to 375°F/190°C and slide the baking tray onto the heated tiles. Bake for 15–20 minutes. Rotate the tray after 10 minutes to ensure the dough browns evenly. It doesn't seem like a long baking time, but these breads are traditionally eaten while the dough is soft and sticks ever so slightly to the teeth, rather than thoroughly dried out. While the bread is baking, mix together the glaze ingredients except the almonds; it should be fairly runny.

FINISHING

Slide the bread and the baking paper onto a pair of cooling racks set side by side – it is a large loaf. Brush lightly with the soft, warm icing – it is a glaze rather than a thick coating – and sprinkle the toasted almonds over the top. Once the bread is cool, use a spatula to loosen it from the baking paper and slide the loaf onto a large serving tray or board. I usually sift icing sugar over Swedish Coffee Bread before serving it. You should get at least 40 slices out of it.

‡ **Ojakangas, Beatrice, *The Great Scandinavian Baking Book*, Little Brown and Co., Boston, Mass., 1988, page 84.**

Yorkshire Parkin

INGREDIENTS

¾ lb	**flour**	**340 g**
½ oz	**ground ginger**	**4 tsp**
grating	**nutmeg**	**grating**
½ lb	**oatmeal***	**225 g**
½ lb	**brown sugar**	**225 g**
2 oz	**mixed peel**	**55 g**
2 oz	**preserved ginger**	**55 g**
½ lb	**butter**	**225 g**
¾ lb	**treacle**	**340 g**
1 tsp	**baking soda**	**1 tsp**
¼ cup	**milk**	**3 tbsp**
2	**eggs, beaten**	**2**

* I used rolled oats, but try oatmeal if you can find some

** teacup

YORKSHIRE COOKERY

The key ingredients for Yorkshire Parkin are treacle, oatmeal and ginger with varying quantities of butter or lard, flour, sugar and milk and sometimes an egg or two. It sounds unexciting, but like much traditional baking Parkin has a strangely addictive simplicity. It keeps very well and is best left for a day or two before cutting. I like most kinds of gingerbread but the nubbly rolled oats and sticky-on-your-teeth taste of treacle make this one a particular favourite. (There are no recipes in *A Yorkshire Cookery Book* for Yorkshire Pudding – obviously everyone already knew how to make it.)

I have a 1917 copy of *A Yorkshire Cookery Book*, with a drawing of the white rose of York on the cover, which includes 17 different recipes for Parkin. The book was compiled by Mary Milnes Gaskell and proceeds from sales were 'Devoted to the purchase of Materials for Soldiers' Garments, both at the Front and in Hospital'. Somewhat daunted by all those recipes I turned to this version of Parkin which was contributed by Mrs Tythe-Brown of Hataitai to *The Ideal Cookery Book* compiled by Ethel M. Cameron in aid of the Funds of the Plunket Society (Wellington Branch), 1933. Large squares of Parkin should be served on Guy Fawkes' Night – or eaten with a cup of tea any time at all.

GETTING READY

Preheat the oven to 340°F/170°C. Grease a 9 in/23 cm square tin and line the base with baking paper. Chop the preserved ginger, warm together the butter and treacle, and dissolve the baking soda in the milk.

MIXING AND BAKING

1. Sift the flour and spices into a large bowl, and add the oatmeal or rolled oats followed by the brown sugar, mixed peel and ginger.
2. Stir in the butter and treacle, then the baking soda and milk and mix well. It will be a heavy mixture. Set aside for about 30 minutes. (Mrs Tythe-Brown suggests several hours if you are using oatmeal.)
3. Mix in the eggs and, when everything is well combined, scoop it into the prepared tin and smooth the top. Bake for at least 60 minutes, rotating after 30 minutes. When it is done, the Parkin will have a shiny top and will spring back when pushed lightly with your finger. Store airtight.

Jams and Preserves

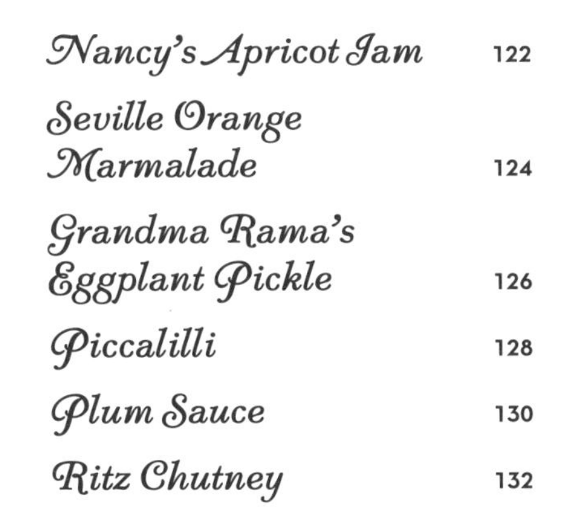

Apricot Jam is enjoyed all over Western and Eastern Europe and North Africa and Seville Orange Marmalade is a famous Scottish recipe (made with Spanish oranges). But the other recipes here owe a great deal to the influence of Indian cooking and spices on British cooking, which began during the time of the Raj and continues unabated to this day.

Ritz Chutney is made from pie melons and, despite its classy London name, it mimics the texture of mango chutney, the famous hot-sweet relish which India exports all over the world. I am pleased to be able to include a very fine Eggplant Pickle recipe from an Indian/New Zealand cook, Mrs Rama, who is a great friend of my friend Myra Lawrie.

Plum Sauce is almost as versatile as Tomato Sauce and can even be used in Asian cooking so, since large crops of plums tend to be more common than surplus tomatoes, Plum Sauce is a useful recipe to have on hand in late summer. I hope this small selection of preserves will give you something to spice up any meal at any time of the day – as well as the snacks in between.

Nancy's Apricot Jam

INGREDIENTS

1 lb	**dried apricots**	**450 g**
5 cups*	**water**	**1125 ml**
5 cups	**sugar**	**1 kg**
2	**lemons**	**2**

* 225 ml cups

Since not all of us are fortunate enough to live in Central Otago where we could enjoy the unparalleled taste of fresh, ripe apricots, we have to make do with the dried variety. Luckily these are available all year round and they make the very best jam with all the concentrated flavour of the dried fruit. Jams need sugar as their preservative so, unless you want to keep them in the fridge, you need a good amount of sugar, but I do not like apricot jam that is too sweet. This recipe is the answer. It comes from Myra Lawrie's sister Nancy Yarndley, the source of the Lemon Loaf on page 68. As with that recipe, Nancy has fine-tuned the amount of sugar to ensure a wonderful tart flavour, a good set and excellent keeping qualities – although it is hard to leave a jar of beautiful apricot jam sitting in the cupboard for long.

GETTING READY

Heat the oven to 300°F/150°C. Wash about 4 jam jars in hot water, rinse them and place in the oven to dry. Put a couple of small saucers in the freezer to use when testing the jam for setting. Squeeze the juice from the lemons.

MAKING THE JAM

1. Chop the apricots into smallish bits and place in a preserving pan with the water. Bring to the boil, stirring, then cover and simmer for 30 minutes.
2. Add the sugar and lemon juice, stir until sugar dissolves and bring the jam to a fast boil, stirring often. It is not a good idea to leave the kitchen when making jam, so have your book at the ready or music on before you start.
3. The jam should take about 20 minutes to reach setting point, but start testing for a set after 10 minutes. Put a drop of jam onto one of your chilled saucers, wait about 15 seconds, then push a finger gently through it. If the surface wrinkles slightly in front of your finger the jam is ready. Turn off the heat, remove the hot jars from the oven and put them on a board.
4. Skim any froth from the top of the jam – or drop in about a teaspoon of butter which, as it melts, magically makes the froth disappear. Ladle the jam into a heatproof jug and pour into the jars. Cover the jars immediately and try not to move them until the jam is cold and set. Label and store in a cool, dark place. Makes about 4 x 400 ml jars.

APRICOT CAKE

Here is another way of enjoying your jam. The recipe was contributed by Bernice Vowell to the *Manawatu Red Cookery Book: Tested and Tried Recipes*, published in Palmerston North in 1926. This was a 'New, Revised and Enlarged Edition' and the copy I have was inscribed by Mrs M.W.M. Stewart on 11 October 1927. Cream 4 oz/115 g butter with 5 oz/140 g sugar; beat in 3 eggs and then fold in 8 oz/225 g flour sifted with 1 tsp baking powder. Lastly stir in 3 tbsp of apricot jam. Bake in a 7 in/18 cm greased and floured tin at 350°F/180°C for about 45 minutes. Ice with lemon icing.

ranny's Apricot Jam
ups 450g Apricots
ups Water boil 1/2hr
an add 5 cups Sugar
oil till set approx 1/2hr
2 lemons
Apricot Jam
Apricot Jam 04/09
04/09
04/09

Seville Orange Marmalade

INGREDIENTS

2 lb	**Seville oranges**	**1 kg**
2 lb	**sugar**	**1 kg**

New Zealand cookery books generally have at least three recipes for marmalade (and sometimes as many as 10), made from various combinations of grapefruit, sweet oranges and lemons, and bitter oranges – also called 'poorman's oranges'. The fruit is usually minced or sliced, then boiled up or soaked overnight to soften the peel before boiling again with sugar. I remember helping my father put grapefruit and lemons through the mincer on the Kenwood Chef, since in our family, as in many others, making marmalade was a man's job. I now prefer Seville oranges, which are very bitter indeed and were used in the first citrus marmalade, which seems to have originated in Scotland. A few are commercially grown in New Zealand, but I have planted a tree to ensure a good supply. This recipe, based on one by British food historian Alan Davidson and included in his book of essays *A Kipper with My Tea*, makes a wonderfully tart marmalade with a beautiful colour, but if you follow the instructions below you can substitute any combination of citrus that pleases you.* As well as eating it on your breakfast toast, use some in the Marmalade Tea Loaf on page 98.

PREPARING THE FRUIT

1. Wash the fruit, cut it into quarters, put in a preserving pan and add enough water to cover them. They'll float, but make sure you have plenty of liquid. Bring to the boil, cover to reduce evaporation, and simmer for about 1 hour until you can pierce the peel with a fine skewer. It won't get any softer after you add the sugar, so make sure it's as tender as you want it to be.
2. Drain the fruit and return the juice to the preserving pan. Once the fruit is cool enough to handle, scrape the flesh and seeds away from the peels – a sharp-edged spoon is good for this, or a peach-pitter. Put this pulp back into the pan with the juice and boil it all for 10 minutes while you slice the peels as thickly or thinly as you wish.

MAKING THE MARMALADE

1. Heat the oven to 300°F/150°C. Wash about 8 jam jars in hot water, rinse them and put them to drain and dry in the oven. Put a couple of small saucers into the freezer – you'll use them to test the marmalade for setting.
2. Pour the liquid from the preserving pan through a sieve, pushing with a wooden spoon to extract as much of the thick juice as you can (it contains the pectin that will make the marmalade set). Discard

the contents of the sieve, rinse out the preserving pan and return to it the juice and sliced peels. Bring this to a simmer, add the sugar, stir until the sugar dissolves and increase the heat to bring it to a rolling boil. Watch the marmalade closely to make sure it doesn't boil over and stir it occasionally with a wooden spoon.

3. Start testing for a set after 5 minutes. To do this, put a drop of marmalade onto one of your chilled saucers, wait about 15 seconds, then push a finger gently through it. When the surface wrinkles slightly in front of your finger it is ready. Turn off the heat, remove the hot jars from the oven and put them on a board.

4. Skim any froth from the top of the marmalade and let it sit for 5 minutes to cool and thicken slightly. This ensures that the peel will not rise to the top of the jars. Now ladle the marmalade into a heatproof jug and pour into the jars. Cover the jars immediately and try not to move them until the marmalade is cold and set. Label and store in a cool, dark place. Makes about 8 x 400 ml jars.

• **Alan Davidson, 'Marmalade: an Unpublished Letter to *The Times*' in *A Kipper with My Tea*, Macmillan, London, 1988, page 75. Roger Blackley gave me this delightful book in 1990.**

Grandma Rama's Eggplant Pickle

INGREDIENTS

2 lb	**eggplant**	**1 kg**
4 tbsp	**salt**	**4 tbsp**
1 cup	**vegetable oil**	**225 ml**
4 oz	**garlic**	**115 g**
4 oz	**root ginger**	**115 g**
2 cups	**vinegar**	**450 ml**
1 cup	**brown sugar**	**200 g**
2 cups	**sultanas**	**280 g**
2 tbsp	**chilli powder**	**2 tbsp**

NOTE

At first sight Myra Lawrie thought my pickle was a little too dry – Grandma Rama's is oilier – but I breathed a sigh of relief when she said the taste was perfect. The reason for the dryness was probably that I cut the eggplant into quite small pieces so it absorbed more of the oil.

Myra Lawrie gave me this recipe, which came from her great friend Mrs Ganga Rama. The Rama family has run an exemplary greengrocer's shop on Auckland's Jervois Road for more than 60 years, and Myra and Ganga have known each other since the 1940s. It is a quickly and easily made Indian preserve and in Myra's words: 'A beautiful pickle and delicious with anything – even on a piece of toast.' I agree.

GETTING READY

Cut the washed, unpeeled eggplant into 1 cm cubes, wearing rubber gloves to stop your fingers from being stained. Sprinkle the salt over the eggplant in a colander and leave for one hour. Meanwhile, peel and coarsely chop the ginger, peel the garlic, and reduce them both to a paste with a couple of tablespoons of water in a blender or food processor.

MAKING THE PICKLE

1. Rinse the eggplant in cold water and squeeze it out well. Discard the liquid.
2. Put the oil in a large pan over a low heat, add the garlic/ginger paste and cook it, stirring, for 1 minute. Add the eggplant and all the remaining ingredients and cook over a low heat for 20 minutes, stirring.
3. Leave the pickle in the pot until it is quite cold, then pour into clean jars and cover. There is no need to sterilise the jars as you would for jam-making as the pickle should be eaten within a couple of weeks. Store in the fridge.

Piccalilli

INGREDIENTS

3 lb	**marrow***	**1.5kg**
1 lb	**cauliflower**	**500 g**
1 lb	**green beans**	**500 g**
½ lb	**onions**	**250 g**
1 small	**cucumber**	**250 g**
1 cup	**salt**	**1 cup**
2 quarts	**vinegar**	**2.4 litres**
2 oz	**flour**	**6 tbsp**
1½ oz	**mustard powder**	**6 tbsp**
1½ oz	**ground ginger**	**6 tbsp**
½ oz	**turmeric**	**2 tbsp**
6 oz	**sugar**	**170 g**

*** You can substitute courgettes for marrow and alter the proportions of the other vegetables to suit your taste. Just make sure the total weight after preparing the vegetables is about 6 lb/3 kg.**

One of the earliest recorded sightings of a recipe for a mustard-yellow, ginger-flavoured, slightly thickened vegetable pickle was apparently in Hannah Glasse's *The Art of Cookery Made Plain and Easy*, published in 1747 and incorporating many recipes from earlier sources. More than two centuries later it is still being made and, judging by the number of recipes for it in New Zealand cookery books, we have always enjoyed it. My grandmother Tommie McArtney was a great lover of chutneys and sauces and especially of Piccalilli. There were always several jars of it in her cupboard. She lived to be a very fit and alert 97-year-old, made sure she had a good range of sharply flavoured condiments with her meals, and had great faith in the health-giving powers of a spoonful of cider vinegar taken every day. But to my eternal regret I don't have the recipe for her Piccalilli, so I've had to rely on other sources. This recipe comes from an unnamed contributor to an Aunt Daisy cookbook and the results are very similar to my memory of my grandmother's. Chopped up and layered into a sandwich with a slice of corned beef or cheese, it can't be beaten.

NOTE

In the recipes I looked at, for every 2 quarts/2.4 litres of vinegar, the quantity of flour varied from 1 tbsp to 1 cup/125 g and the quantity of sugar from none to 1 cup/200 g. So sweetness and thickness are a matter of personal taste, and the same goes for spices. The powdered mustard is always there of course, since it's a mustard pickle, but some recipes include curry powder, allspice and cayenne, and some have no ginger. Develop your own brand.

GETTING READY

The day before you make the Piccalilli, trim the beans, peel the cucumber and cut all the vegetables into similar-sized smallish pieces and sprinkle them well with the salt. Cover.

NB: You will be cooking them quickly in vinegar and some modern recipes suggest keeping the onions and cauliflower separate from the beans, courgettes and cucumber, which will need less time in the pot. I don't think my grandmother would have bothered, but it's not a bad idea.

MAKING THE PICKLE

1. After 24 hours, drain the liquid from the vegetables, rinse them and drain again. Heat the oven to 300°F/150°C. Wash about 12 x 400 ml jam jars in hot water, rinse them and put them to drain and dry in the oven.
2. Mix 1 cup of the vinegar with the flour and spices to make a thin, smooth paste and set aside. Put the sugar and the rest of the vinegar into a large preserving pan and bring it to a simmer.
3. Add the vegetables and boil until they are just cooked, but with a hint of crunch left – about 7 minutes. Stir in the spice paste and boil for another 3 minutes, stirring all the time. Spoon into heated jars and cover. Store in a cool, dark place, and leave for two weeks before eating. The pickle will keep for at least a year. Makes 12 x 400 ml jars.

Piccalilli
Piccalilli
04/09
Piccalilli

Plum Sauce

INGREDIENTS

5 lb	**red-fleshed plums**	**2.3 kg**
2 lb	**sugar**	**900 g**
3 pints	**malt vinegar**	**1.8 litres**
4 oz	**garlic**	**115 g**
6 tsp	**salt**	**6 tsp**
2 tsp	**cayenne pepper***	**2 tsp**
2 tsp	**ground cloves**	**2 tsp**
2 tsp	**ground ginger**	**2 tsp**
2 tsp	**ground pepper**	**2 tsp**
	a few blades of mace	

* **Or use 2 whole red chillies, fresh or dried; 2 tsp whole cloves; a slightly crushed thumb-sized piece of fresh ginger; 2 tsp whole black peppercorns and a few blades of mace – all tied into a small square of muslin.**

I made the sauce in the photographs with beautiful Satsuma plums from my friend Jenny Maidment's tree and following a recipe from my mother's copy of the Women's Institutes *Home Cookery Book*, published around 1945. I particularly like this recipe since it contains plenty of garlic and the lack of onions seems to give it a sweeter, more complex flavour. The original recipe suggests using ground spices and adding them to the pan, but I prefer to use whole ones and tie them in a small piece of muslin. That way the spices can be removed when they have done their job of flavouring the sauce and it keeps its plummy red colour.

GETTING READY

Cut the plums in half horizontally and remove the stones. A peach-pitting tool, like a pointed teaspoon with two sharp edges, is good for this. I use an old one that belonged to my father.

COOKING THE SAUCE

1. Put all the ingredients in a preserving pan – not a copper one – and bring the mixture to the boil, stirring. Simmer steadily for about an hour, stirring occasionally, until it has, as my book tells me, reduced to a 'plup'.
2. Remove the spice bag, if using, and force the mixture through a colander or Mouli, or whiz it in batches in the food processor. Allow the sauce to cool in a bowl with a cloth over it.
3. Heat the oven to 300°F/150°C, wash about 6 x 500 ml bottles in hot water, rinse them and place in the oven to dry. Pour the sauce into the heated glass bottles and seal. Store in a cool, dark place. Makes about 12 cups/3 litres.

Plum Sauce
20/1/09
Plum Sauce
20/1/09
Plum Sauce
20/1/09
Plum Sauce
20/1/09

Ritz Chutney

INGREDIENTS

9 lb	**pie melon***	**4 kg**
OR		
9 lb	**feijoas***	**4 kg**
6 lb	**brown sugar**	**2.5 kg**
1 lb	**dates**	**450 g**
4 oz	**garlic**	**115 g**
2½ pints	**malt vinegar**	**1.5 litres**
1 lb	**sultanas**	**450 g**
3 oz	**salt**	**60 g**
1 oz	**dried red chillies**	**30 g**

* You will need to start with 11 lb/5 kg of fruit in order to get 9 lb /4 kg of prepared fruit.

These spherical green melons, with creamy-white, almost tasteless flesh and lots of reddish seeds, once grew in profusion around New Zealand and were used only for chutney and jam. They are hard to find today, but if you track down a supply, you'll find that the shreds of melon cook to a pretty translucence and the flavour is excellent – so good, in fact, that Pie Melon Chutney is called Ritz Chutney in all the Women's Institutes cookery books.

The long British sojourn in the Indian subcontinent resulted in hundreds of recipes for chutneys – combinations of seasonal fruits and vegetables cooked with spices, sugar and vinegar to a pulpy consistency and served with cold meats or bread and cheese. They bear little relation to the original Indian *chatni*, which means a spicy relish freshly made for each meal, but they have a firm place in the cuisines of most former British colonies and are a way of using up whatever fruit or vegetables are in good supply. This one is based on my grandmother's recipe for Melon Chutney, which came from her friend Sis Barstow, and the melon they used was pie melon. I have also made this recipe successfully with feijoas when we have a large crop.

GETTING READY

Cut up the melon, slice off the rind and cut away the central seedy bit, then shred the flesh on the grating attachment of your food processor. My grandmother used her Spong shredder, a rotary grater. Or top and tail the feijoas and slice them finely. The peel cooks well and contributes a pleasant, slightly gritty feel to the finished chutney. Put the fruit into a bowl with the sugar, mix well, cover and leave overnight.

COOKING THE CHUTNEY

1. Put the chopped dates, peeled garlic and some of the vinegar (about ½ cup) into the food processor and reduce to a rough paste. Pour the reserved fruit and sugar into a preserving pan and add the date paste, sultanas, salt, the remaining vinegar and the chillies. My grandmother tied the chillies in a piece of muslin and removed the bag when the chutney was cooked, but I just toss them in.
2. Mix everything well together with a wooden spoon, cover and cook slowly for 2–3 hours, stirring from time to time, until thick and jammy. The chutney is ready when the liquid is mostly evaporated and the fruit seems caramelised. Allow it to cool, covered with a cloth.
3. Ladle the cooled chutney into clean jars, cover, seal and leave for a month before eating. Stored in a cool, dark place it will keep for at least a year. Makes about 15 x 400 ml jars.

Chutney (Dis Barstow
(cut up as for jam
sugar
... garlic a few at a time
... of the vinegar & put in
... equidiser (Kenwood)
... (I use my Spong
... I cover with the brown
... out 24 hours - a plastic
... this
... sultanas salt & the
... garlic & remaining
... preserving pan
... a boil all
... Takes from 2 to 3
... in usual way
NATIONAL
PRESERVING
WAX

Sweets

NOTE

Don't hurry the 'Getting Ready' stage of sweet recipes. You will need to work quickly once the sugar reaches the right temperature, so avoid last-minute dramas by making sure you have everything measured and neatly laid out before you start. You probably won't make these recipes very often, so it is a mistake to rely on memory or risk wasting your time and ingredients by going at it in a slapdash manner. Remember also that a damp room or a steamy day is not suitable for making sweets – especially Hokey Pokey. If you have a sugar thermometer, use it as a backup, but you can mostly test the readiness of the sweet mixtures without one.

In my memories of childhood school fairs, two images loom large. The first is of trestle tables covered with white newsprint bearing long rows of floral sand saucers, all labelled with the names and classrooms of their young creators, and with notices of the prizes awarded in each age group. I was always a keen entrant – but I don't think I ever won anything. My second image is of the sweet stall with its little crêpe paper-covered baskets and paper or cellophane bags filled with delicious assortments of delicacies like Chocolate Fudge, Russian Fudge, pink and white Coconut Ice and Hokey Pokey. Here was guaranteed consolation for sand-saucer disappointments.

We rarely made sweets at home, so despite occasional enthusiastic attempts – mainly at Hokey Pokey – my sisters and I never built up enough experience to be confident sweet-makers. And until recently this situation still stood, since, although I bake a lot, confectionery has not been my forté. Nonetheless, for this book I decided to try to master a few of the classic recipes and I am very pleased with the results.

For the sake of our teeth, sweets should be an occasional treat rather than a daily pleasure, so tape the pages of this chapter closed, if you must – but slit them open every now and then and indulge yourself. Then if you are called on to help stock a community sweet stall you will be ready to meet the challenge. And we have a long tradition to uphold here. I like the picture summoned up by 'Christabel', writing in the 'Social Gossip' column of the *New Zealand Freelance* on 4 June 1906. She noted that St Peter's Exhibition and Fair had been opened the previous Tuesday by His Excellency the Governor, accompanied by Lady Plunket, and that the sweet stall, draped in green and gold, 'did excellent business in pretty baskets of home-made sweets'.

Marshmallows

FOR THE MARSHMALLOW

3 dsp	**gelatine**	**6 tsp**
9 oz	**sugar**	**255 g**
½ pint	**hot water**	**300 ml**
pinch	**cream of tartar**	**pinch**
1	**egg white**	**1**
2 tbsp	**lemon juice**	**2 tbsp**
1 tsp	**vanilla essence**	**1 tsp**
1 tsp	**rosewater***	**1 tsp**
OR		
1 tsp	**orange-flower water***	**1 tsp**

* traditional flavourings, but optional

FOR FINISHING

1 cup	**dessicated coconut***	**85 g**
OR		
4 tbsp	**cornflour**	**40 g**
1 cup	**icing sugar**	**120 g**

* To toast the coconut stir it over a low heat in a dry frying pan for about 3 minutes until it turns a pale golden brown. Watch it carefully as it burns quickly.

Marshmallow is not complicated to make – as you will discover if you make the Marshmallow Slice on page 40. It is simply sugar syrup beaten with soaked gelatine and an egg white, so you could make the Marshmallow Slice topping, pour it into a tin and cut it up for marshmallow sweets. But this recipe, for which I recommend using a sugar thermometer, gives a superior result – a firmer, more resilient marshmallow – created by boiling the sugar syrup to a higher temperature. The choice is up to you and both recipes work well.

GETTING READY

You will need a heavy-based, straight-sided saucepan, preferably 5 in/12 cm deep and a sugar thermometer or a bowl of cold water and a wooden chopstick for testing. Line the base and two sides of a shallow 12 x 8 in/30 x 21cm tin with baking paper, taking it far enough up the sides to allow you to lift the marshmallow out later. Combine the flavourings in a cup.

MAKING THE MARSHMALLOW

1. Put the gelatine into a small bowl with 2 tbsp cool water, or enough to make the gelatine swell – there shouldn't be any dry bits left. Set aside. Put the sugar, hot water and cream of tartar into the saucepan and bring slowly to the boil, stirring to make sure the sugar dissolves completely before the mixture boils. To test it, I dip a wooden chopstick into the syrup, then rub the syrup between wet fingertips to feel whether any sugar granules remain.
2. Clip the sugar thermometer onto the side of the saucepan and boil gently for 15–20 minutes until the temperature reaches 260°F/130°C. If you drop a little syrup into cold water it will form a firm ball which will hold its shape but is still pliable.
3. While the syrup is simmering, beat the egg white until stiff and set it aside. Put the swelled gelatine into a larger bowl and have your electric mixer ready. If you have a stand mixer, use the whisk attachment.
4. When the syrup is ready pour it onto the gelatine. Add the flavourings and begin to beat the mixture hard. After about a minute, stop beating and add the egg white, then beat again until the mixture is cold, very white and very fluffy. You can add a little colouring if you wish.

5. Pour the marshmallow into the tin, level the top and put it aside to set. After 12 hours at room temperature it will be completely set and the top will be dry to the touch. You could speed it up slightly in the fridge, but the longer setting time makes the marshmallow firmer and easier to cut into shapes.

FINISHING

1. Turn the slab of marshmallow out onto a board and carefully peel away the baking paper. For coconut squares, cut the marshmallow with a hot, dry knife and roll the pieces in plain or toasted coconut. For plain marshmallows, cut the mixture into squares, or shapes with a biscuit cutter, and roll them in the sifted cornflour and icing sugar mixture.
2. Once the marshmallows are firm and dry, store airtight. (If you use cutters you will have some bits left over. You could just eat them or add up to 3 oz/85 g to the Creamy Chocolate Fudge on page 142.)

Coconut Ice

INGREDIENTS FOR EACH LAYER

1½ cups	**caster sugar**	**300 g**
½ cup*	**milk**	**110 ml**
½ oz	**butter**	**15 g**
⅔ cup	**coconut**	**65 g**
½ tsp	**coconut essence**	**½ tsp**

*** small**

FOR A PINK LOWER LAYER

½ tsp	**coconut essence**	**½ tsp**
2 drops	**red food colouring**	**2 drops**

FOR A GREEN LOWER LAYER

¼ tsp	**peppermint essence**	**¼ tsp**
2 drops	**green food colouring**	**2 drops**

Having tried in vain to achieve a two-layer, pink-and-white coconut ice by colouring the second half of the mixture after pouring the first half into the tin, I decided to make it in two separate batches – and it worked. I also add a little coconut essence, which ups the coconut factor considerably and makes the whole confection a fractionally less sugary experience. The green and white version has a tiny bit of peppermint essence in the lower layer and this works well, too.

GETTING READY

You will need a heavy-based, straight-sided saucepan, preferably 5 in/12 cm deep; a simmer mat; a metal whisk with a heatproof handle; a bowl of cold water and a long-handled spoon or wooden chopstick for testing. Grease a 6 in/16 cm square tin and line it with a piece of baking paper, taking it far enough up the sides to allow you to lift out the Coconut Ice later. Measure out the essence and food colouring and mix it in an eggcup ready to add.

MAKING THE COCONUT ICE

1. Put the sugar, milk and butter in the saucepan on a simmer mat over a very gentle heat and stir. The sugar must be totally dissolved before the mixture comes to the boil (3–5 minutes). To test it, I dip a wooden chopstick into the syrup, then rub the syrup between wet fingertips to feel whether any sugar granules remain.
2. Once you have a smooth, whitish syrup, increase the heat very slightly and bring the mixture to a gentle boil, stirring constantly with the metal whisk as the temperature rises. Test after it has boiled for 2 minutes by dropping some of the mixture into the bowl of cold water and keep testing until it forms a soft ball between your fingers (238°F/114°C).
3. Remove the saucepan to a heatproof mat, tip in the coconut and the essence and colouring, and stir gently for 1–2 minutes until the mixture just begins to thicken and become opaque. Pour it into the tin and make the second layer in the same way, but without the colouring. Pour it on top of the first.
4. After a few minutes, score it lightly with a knife into squares. Give it another 15 minutes or so then, while it is still warm, lift out the whole slab using the baking paper and cut it carefully along the marked lines. The Coconut Ice will still seem slightly damp, so set out the squares on a baking tray and allow them to dry. Store airtight.

Hokey Pokey

INGREDIENTS

6 tbsp	**sugar**	**115 g**
4 tbsp	**golden syrup**	**115 g**
1 tsp	**baking soda**	**1 tsp**

Although some British recipe books have recipes for Hokey Pokey, they seem usually to be made using caramelised sugar, without the essential golden syrup that gives Antipodean Hokey Pokey its delicious crunchy stickiness. This is our classic recipe; it needs no alteration.

GETTING READY

You will need a heavy-based, straight-sided saucepan, preferably 5 in/12 cm deep and a simmer mat. Grease a shallow metal tin with butter and sift the baking soda through a tea strainer into a cup.

MAKING THE HOKEY POKEY

1. Put the sugar and golden syrup in the saucepan on a simmer mat over gentle heat and bring them slowly to the boil, stirring constantly with a wooden spoon. The sugar will take about 6 minutes to dissolve.
2. Continue to simmer over a very low heat, stirring. After about 4 minutes the syrup should be a very dark gold and smell faintly of caramel – not like burned sugar.
3. Remove the saucepan from the stove and put it on a heatproof surface. Drop in the baking soda and mix quickly with the wooden spoon. The mixture will fluff up dramatically. Keep stirring until the soda is all incorporated, with no white streaks. In a few seconds it will turn a paler gold and be very frothy. Tip it quickly into the greased tin and leave it the way it falls – if you try to spread it out you will crush the bubbles that give it its honeycomb centre.
4. Leave the Hokey Pokey for about 30 minutes to harden and cool completely before breaking it up into shards. Store airtight, but try to eat it within 24 hours or stickiness will take over from crunchiness.

Russian Fudge

INGREDIENTS

1lb 4oz	**caster sugar**	**565 g**
½ cup	**milk**	**125 ml**
4 oz	**butter**	**115 g**
3 tbsp	**golden syrup**	**3 tbsp**
½ tin	**sweetened condensed milk**	**200 g**
2 tsp	**vanilla essence**	**2 tsp**

After compiling a spreadsheet of 16 slightly different recipes for this confection dating from 1934 to 2009 – half of which called it Russian Toffee (and one was Swiss Fudge); and after consulting Richard Smith, a friend who is something of a Russian Fudge czar; and after much testing and slow stirring (while listening to slow Russian music), I believe I have achieved nirvana. This recipe has less sugar than many others, which helps prevent the finished fudge from being too hard and crystalline, so if you follow my instructions *to the letter* you will end up with a tray of caramel-coloured, creamy-smooth fudge. If you like Russian Fudge I suggest you put on some stirring music and prepare to make a New Zealand and Australian classic. (I don't think the Russians have ever heard of it.)

GETTING READY

You will need a heavy-based, straight-sided saucepan, preferably 5 in/12 cm deep; a simmer mat; a metal whisk with a heatproof handle; a bowl of cold water and a long-handled spoon or wooden chopstick for testing. I use a hand-held electric mixer to beat the fudge while it is cooling but a wooden spoon will do it. Grease an 8 in/21 cm square tin and line it with a piece of baking paper. Chop the butter into small lumps.

MAKING THE FUDGE

1. Put the sugar and milk in the saucepan on a simmer mat over a very gentle heat and stir. The sugar must be totally dissolved before the mixture comes to the boil (this can take up to 10 minutes). To test it, I dip a wooden chopstick into the syrup, then rub the syrup between wet fingertips to feel whether any sugar granules remain.
2. Once you have a smooth whitish syrup, add the butter, golden syrup and sweetened condensed milk and stir until they blend. Increase the heat very slightly and bring the mixture to a gentle boil,

stirring constantly with the metal whisk as the temperature slowly rises. Stirring helps give the fudge a creamy consistency and also stops it from burning. (Sweetened condensed milk burns with horrible ease.) Test after 8 minutes by dropping some of the mixture into the bowl of cold water and keep testing every minute or so until it forms a soft ball between your fingers (238°F/114°C).

3. When the moment comes, pour the fudge into a large heatproof bowl, preferably ceramic. Add the vanilla, stir it in and leave to cool for 2–3 minutes. Now start beating with your beater, or wooden spoon. The fudge will begin to thicken after 2–3 minutes, but should still level out when you take out the beaters, so stop and check every 30 seconds or so. When it is the consistency of thick custard or porridge and still hot, pour it into the prepared tin. A heatproof silicone scraper is a help with this. Leave it to cool for about 15 minutes, then mark into squares. Cut up when cool and set (after about an hour). It will become firmer as it cools completely.

FUDGE FAILURES

I now believe my childhood fudge failures were usually caused by boiling the mixture for too long so it began to set and crystallise almost as soon as the pot came off the stove. It is important to test the mixture regularly – and I do this even though I have a sugar thermometer – once it has been gently boiling for 8 minutes or so. It may take 15 or 20 minutes to reach 238°F/114°C or the soft-ball stage, so be patient. I dip a wooden chopstick into the syrup, then put it into cold water and test the syrup between my fingertips. Remember you are after a soft ball that barely holds its shape, not a firm ball. If the fudge doesn't thicken and become creamy as you beat it, you may have stopped boiling too soon, but you can always reboil it – a trick Richard Smith told me. The same applies if you have boiled it for too long. Scrape it back into the pot, add a few tablespoons of milk to soften it and bring back to the boil, stirring all the time.

Creamy Chocolate Fudge

INGREDIENTS

1¾ cups	sugar	350 g
½ tin	evaporated milk	200 ml
2 oz	butter	55 g
6 oz	dark chocolate	170 g
2 oz	walnuts*	55 g
1 tsp	vanilla essence	1 tsp

* coarsely chopped

I was always a little disappointed with the crumbly, sugary chocolate fudge I made as a young cook, despite it being the norm at sweet stalls and parties. So here is a different kind of fudge, based on an American recipe which uses chocolate rather than cocoa. It is a very creamy, firm fudge and I hope you'll agree that it is an improvement on tradition.

GETTING READY

You will need a heavy-based, straight-sided saucepan, preferably 5 in/12 cm deep; a simmer mat; a metal whisk with a heatproof handle; a bowl of cold water and a long-handled spoon or wooden chopstick for testing. Reduce the chocolate to crumbs in a food processor, or chop it very finely with a knife. Put the butter and chocolate into a large mixing bowl. Grease an 8 in/20 cm square tin and line it with a piece of baking paper.

MAKING THE FUDGE

1. Put the sugar and evaporated milk in the saucepan on a simmer mat over a low heat and stir until the sugar has dissolved completely (about 5 minutes). To test it, I dip a wooden chopstick into the syrup, then rub the syrup between wet fingertips to feel whether any sugar granules remain. Now simmer the syrup gently, stirring all the time, for 6 minutes (the temperature will now be near 238°F/114°C). If any small brownish bits appear, the syrup is beginning to catch on the bottom of the pan – they will disappear when you add the chocolate.
2. Pour the caramel-coloured syrup onto the butter and chocolate, and mix with a wooden spoon or silicone scraper until thick and smooth. (If you are adding some marshmallow to the fudge – see page 136 – combine it with the chocolate and butter and it will melt into the mixture. Marshmallow makes the fudge a little smoother, but also a little sweeter.) Add the walnuts and vanilla and when everything is combined tip it quickly into the prepared tin and smooth the top with a few swirling strokes of the silicone scraper. Don't dab at the surface too much or the top will lose its gloss. Set it aside to cool a little, then mark into squares with a knife.
3. Once the fudge is cold, refrigerate it for about an hour to set firmly, then cut it into squares, put the squares on a tray and set aside for about 2 hours so the edges become quite firm. Store airtight – in the fridge if the weather is very warm.

Kokila's Chocolate Truffles

INGREDIENTS

1 pkt	**super wine biscuits**	**250 g**
½ cup	**caster sugar**	**100 g**
8 tsp	**cocoa powder**	**8 tsp**
3½ oz	**unsalted butter**	**100 g**
4 tbsp	**brandy***	**60 ml**

* or orange juice

FINISHING

1 cup	**dessicated coconut**	**85 g**

Home-made truffles are often very rich, when made with chocolate, cream and egg yolks; or very sweet, when made with various combinations of dried fruit, icing sugar, butter and sometimes milk powder. I seldom like them very much so I was delighted when my cousin Kokila Patel brought these little truffles to our family Christmas last year. They are not too sweet, not too rich, with just the right amount of brandy for a festive flavour, and they keep well and look pretty. When Kokila kindly sent me the recipe, I realised they are really a truffle version of the famous New Zealand biscuit fudge cake. No wonder they are so popular.

GETTING READY

Crush the biscuits to very fine crumbs in a food processor, or put them in a plastic bag and beat them with a rolling pin. Sift the cocoa and have the butter very soft at room temperature.

MAKING THE TRUFFLES

1. Combine the biscuit crumbs, sugar and sifted cocoa in a large mixing bowl. Add the butter and mix it through, using your hand and squeezing everything together.
2. Pour in the brandy or orange juice a little at a time, still kneading and squeezing the mixture. It will seem too crumbly and dry at first, but persevere and as the biscuit crumbs absorb the brandy, the mixture will come together into a soft, pliable mass. You should have a clean bowl at the end and your hands should not be too messy. Keep kneading until you reach this point.
3. Use a measuring teaspoon to scoop out small dabs of the mixture. Roll them into balls, then roll them in coconut. Place on a tray or plate and refrigerate to firm up, then serve in a pretty bowl. They will keep for several days. Makes 60 small truffles.

NOTE

You could vary the flavour by replacing some of the brandy with a fruit liqueur, but don't go overboard. The simplicity of these truffles is a big part of their charm.

Savouries

Inside a large black handwritten recipe book, among dozens of newspaper clippings and extra recipes written on scraps of paper and the backs of letters, I found a cutting from the *Dominion* of Saturday, 9 April 1960. The column was called 'Susan's Week' and the headline reads 'Versatile "Dip" is New Food Idea for Parties'. The columnist acknowledges that New Zealand home cooks are famous for their desserts but today, she suggests:

> let's concentrate on appetising 'befores' instead of delicious 'afters'; in a word let's concentrate on that wonderful American invention, the dip. The joy of a dip is its versatility. You can dress up a very fancy one of gourmet ingredients to be the star turn at a cocktail party. But equally well you can whisk up a very simple and inexpensive one in the proverbial jiffy.

So I decided dips it would be in this chapter, as well as some very good fillings for dainty sandwiches and pinwheel scones, and two other savouries of the kind that appear in the 'Some Cheese Notions' chapter of the Women's Institutes *Home Cookery Book*. With these at the ready, the 'befores' can be just as exciting as the 'afters' at every party.

The black recipe book was lent to me by Katherine Habershon. It belonged to her Auntie Eve – Evelyn Matthews, who was for many years the cook at the Heretaunga Golf Club in Lower Hutt. Although Miss Matthews's book is like a time capsule of old recipes, she was clearly still interested in new ideas. The golfers of Heretaunga must have been very well looked after.

Versatile Dips

INGREDIENTS

1 ctn*	**cream cheese**	**250 g**
1 wedge	**blue vein cheese**	**100 g**
2½ oz	**butter**	**70 g**
1 dsp	**brandy or port**	**2 tsp**
lots of	**ground black pepper**	**2 tsp**
3 dashes	**Tabasco**	**½ tsp**
2 tbsp	**chopped parsley****	**2 tbsp**
2 tbsp	**cream****	**2 tbsp**

* carton
** optional

BLUE VEIN DIP

When I went to work at Auckland City Art Gallery in 1978, there existed a group of people called the Art Gallery Associates, which had been founded in the 1950s. They later changed their name to Friends of the Auckland Art Gallery, an appropriate reflection of their continuing contribution to the gallery's life. They organised most of the social functions around the exhibition programme, as well as numerous lectures, talks and concerts – and the standard of catering at their events always ensured a good turnout of gallery staff. The food was provided by members of the committee and once, after realising I was spending far too long stationed beside Liz Fumpston's superlative Blue Vein Dip, I decided to ask her how she made it. Liz was an elegant and lovely woman, who showed no sign of ever having eaten this dip herself, but she kindly gave me the recipe. Here it is.

TO MAKE THE DIP

1. Place all the ingredients in a saucepan and heat gently, stirring with a wooden spoon until almost mixed together. Don't overdo this stage – it shouldn't all be melted, just softened and starting to blend.
2. Scrape into a food processor or blender and process until it is a smooth dip. Add more liquid cream if necessary to get the right consistency. Serve with small biscuits.

INGREDIENTS

8 oz	**cottage cheese**	**225 g**
4 oz	**soft butter**	**115 g**
2 tbsp	**sour cream***	**2 tbsp**
1	**small onion**	**1**
1 tsp	**capers****	**1 tsp**
½ tsp	**salt**	**½ tsp**
1 tbsp	**mustard†**	**1 tbsp**
1½ tsp	**paprika**	**1½ tsp**
1 tsp	**caraway seeds**	**1 tsp**

* Mrs Paykel suggests souring some fresh cream with a few drops of lemon juice
** I increase the capers to 2 tbsp. You could also add some chopped gherkins
† Dijon or hot English

LIPTAUER

A delicious savoury cheese dip, this recipe is from *The Menorah Cookbook: A Selection of Recipes Contributed by the Jewish Women of New Zealand*, published in Auckland in 1964. It came from Mrs E. Paykel. Serve it with vegetable sticks or crackers.

MAKING THE DIP

Cream together the cottage cheese, butter and sour cream until everything is well blended – a food processor does this very efficiently. Scrape the mixture into a bowl. Grate the onion finely and add it with the other ingredients. Mix well. Taste for seasoning and serve sprinkled with more paprika.

INGREDIENTS

1 tin*	**reduced cream**	**250 ml**
1 pkt	**onion soup powder**	**32 g**
1 tsp	**lemon juice**	**1 tsp**

* small tin

CLASSIC NEW ZEALAND DIP

If Blue Vein Dip is a 'star turn', then this one is a 'very simple and inexpensive alternative', and certainly made in the proverbial jiffy. The taste is so familiar and so satisfying that it's hard to believe there are only three ingredients – although two of them are pre-processed – and they work together to create a perfect harmony of taste and texture.

TO MAKE THE DIP

Combine all the ingredients, mix well, cover and chill for 30 minutes before serving.

Cheese Turnovers

INGREDIENTS

1 batch	cream cheese pastry*	1 batch
2 tsp	hot English mustard**	2 tsp
4 oz	tasty cheese	115 g
½ tsp	vinegar	½ tsp
	salt and pepper to taste	

* See recipe page 50
** ready mixed, not powder

NOTE

In her 1954 book *Austrian Cooking and Baking*†, Gretel Beer notes: 'You can also use [cream cheese pastry, page 50] for sausage rolls or – cut into strips, brushed with egg white, sprinkled with coarse salt, paprika and caraway seeds and baked – as a cocktail savoury.' (This last is a great way to use up any leftover cream cheese pastry scraps.)

† Gretel Beer, *Austrian Cooking and Baking*, Andre Deutsch, London, 1954, page 154.

I found this recipe in the *Otago Witness* while researching a book for the Dunedin Public Art Gallery on Frances Hodgkins's paintings. Looking through newspapers on microfilm to find small mentions of your research topic can be exhausting stuff, but if you throw in a quick look at the Women's Pages of the newspaper you are suddenly transported into the world inhabited by your subject – in this case one of New Zealand's greatest painters. I have no idea whether Frances Hodgkins looked to the newspaper for interesting recipes, although she could cook and I do know that she made a Veal and Ham Pie on 20 April 1895 since she mentioned it in a letter to her sister Isabel. But Frances had left New Zealand on her first trip to Europe several weeks before this recipe appeared on 20 March 1901 so, alas, she missed out on Cheese Turnovers. Luckily we can still make them.

GETTING READY

Make the pastry the day before, divide into two rectangles, wrap and refrigerate overnight. Take it out of the fridge and let it sit on the bench for 20 minutes. Preheat the oven to 400°F/200°C. Line a baking tray with baking paper or grease it lightly. Grate the cheese or cut it into thin slices.

ASSEMBLY AND BAKING

1. Roll out one half of the pastry on a floured board to a rectangle about 12 x 7 in/30 x 18 cm. Spread 1 tsp of mustard evenly over one side of the pastry, top with half the cheese, sprinkle ¼ tsp vinegar over and season with salt and pepper.
2. Flip the other side of the pastry over to cover the filling, pinch the edges to seal, prick the top with a fork in a few places, and move the parcel carefully onto the baking tray. Repeat with the other piece of pastry. Refrigerate for 10 minutes.
3. Brush the tops of the turnovers with water and sprinkle with a little flaky salt, then bake for 15 minutes, rotating after 10 minutes. Remove from the oven and leave on the tray for 5 minutes, then slide onto a board and cut each turnover into nine fingers. Serve them warm. (You can leave them in the fridge for several hours before you bake them and then produce them with a flourish when you need them.)

Dainty Sandwiches

INGREDIENTS

1 lb	shin or topside of beef	450 g
1 tsp	salt	1 tsp
1 tsp	ground mace*	1 tsp
1 tsp	black pepper	1 tsp
¼ tsp	cayenne pepper	¼ tsp
2 tbsp	anchovy sauce**	2 tbsp
¼ lb	ham (optional)	115 g
3 oz	butter	85 g

* Mace is sometimes hard to get, but it is a vital contributor to this recipe. I buy it whole from Indian suppliers (it is called *javitri*) and reduce it to a powder in a spice grinder – a coffee grinder which I keep for spices.

** Anchovy sauce appears in most New Zealand recipes for meat paste, as does Worcestershire Sauce (which also contains anchovy). You could substitute anchovy paste from a tube. For a different flavour I sometimes use 2 tbsp brandy or sherry.

NOTE

I think sandwiches look most appetising set out on a white doily on a silver tray – from which they will disappear very quickly.

THREE GOOD SANDWICH FILLINGS

1. HOME-MADE POTTED MEAT PASTE

You should make your own meat paste. All early New Zealand recipe books expect you to. It will bear scant relation to the bought variety that lurks in tiny jars on supermarket shelves and be every bit as delicious as a rich pâté. Just steam some lean beef for two or three hours with a few seasonings, then either put through the mincer twice – if you are being a retrospective cook – or quickly whiz it in the food processor with some melted butter. The simplicity of the ingredients and the process belie the wonderful result. Use on its own in sandwiches or on toast and, as one recipe book promises, 'Your family will love you for this'.

GETTING READY

Find a bowl or a small casserole, with a lid, that will fit inside a large, lidded saucepan. Put an upturned small plate or a trivet in the saucepan. Remove all fat from the beef and chop it into small pieces. Cut up the ham, too, if you are using it, and put it with all the other ingredients, except the butter, into the bowl.

MAKING THE POTTED MEAT PASTE

1. Cover the bowl tightly with a double layer of aluminium foil, and secure with string, or cover the casserole with aluminium foil and put the lid on top to hold it in place. Now stand your meat container in the saucepan with enough water to come halfway up its side and put the lid on the saucepan. Bring to the boil and simmer very gently for 2½–3 hours. Top up the saucepan with boiling water if the level drops.
2. Put the cooked meat and its juices into the food processor and reduce to a paste. When it has cooled a little, gradually add the melted butter.
3. Put into small pots or jars and cover with a little more melted butter to seal it. Store in the fridge, but use at room temperature. It will keep for at least four weeks.

MAKING THE SANDWICHES

For potted meat sandwiches, use one slice of white bread and one of brown. You don't need to butter the bread.

2. MOCK CRAB

Mock Cream, Mock Chicken, Mock Goose and Mock Crab – none of these relate very closely to the dishes they mimic, but they have long been popular in New Zealand and have a homely sort of charm. Mock Chicken and Mock Crab are both sandwich fillings based on seasoned egg. Mock Chicken includes mixed herbs – presumably as a reminder of chicken stuffing – and Mock Crab might not taste of crab, but it looks a little like pink-and-white crab meat and is surprisingly flavoursome. Mock Crab sandwiches should be made with white bread.

INGREDIENTS

2	firm tomatoes	2
2	hard-boiled eggs	2
1 cup*	grated cheese	100 g
1 tsp	lemon juice	1 tsp
pinch	cayenne pepper	pinch
1–2 tsp	mayonnaise**	1–2 tsp
	salt, pepper and Tabasco to taste	

* breakfast cup
** or olive oil

MAKING THE MOCK CRAB

Blanch the tomatoes with boiling water, remove the skins, cut them in half and squeeze out the seeds, then dice the flesh finely. Mix everything together, adding a little mayonnaise or oil to form a rough paste and season well.

MAKING THE SANDWICHES

Spread slices of white bread with softened butter and fill with the mock crab. Remove the crusts and cut the sandwiches into small fingers or triangles using a very sharp knife.

3. LETTUCE ALONE (HONEYMOON SANDWICHES)

Among the most successful sandwiches I have ever made. This inspired combination of mint butter and shredded lettuce on brown bread comes from *Michael Smith's Afternoon Tea*†.

FOR THE MINT BUTTER

6 oz	unsalted butter	170 g
20–24	large mint leaves	20–24
1 tsp	lemon juice	1 tsp
½ tsp	salt	½ tsp
½ tsp	granulated sugar	½ tsp

MAKING THE MINT BUTTER

Have the butter at room temperature and combine with the chopped mint and other ingredients in a food processor to create a soft, green-flecked spread. Michael Smith suggests sieving out the mint leaves but I leave them in. The tiny bit of sugar gives a very satisfying faint crunch.

MAKING THE SANDWICHES

Spread the butter on brown bread, cover with a thin layer of finely shredded lettuce, then top with another slice of mint-buttered bread. Remove the crusts and cut into triangles.

† Smith, Michael, *Michael Smith's Afternoon Tea*, MacMillan, London, 1986, page 79.

Savoury Cheese Dreams

Of these small cheesy tartlets from the 1945 Women's Institutes *Home Cookery Book*, the recipe writer comments: 'These are delightful for suppers, and may be reheated in the oven for a few minutes before serving.' This is another good use for the flaky cream cheese pastry (see page 50) that has become my favourite and like many of these simple recipes it is open to variation – try adding some finely chopped ham, or a little flaked smoked fish and some chopped chives.

INGREDIENTS

½ batch	**cream cheese pastry**	**½ batch**
2 tbsp	**flour**	**20 g**
1 cup	**grated cheese**	**85 g**
1	**egg**	**1**
½ tsp	**hot mustard**	**½ tsp**
1 cup	**milk**	**225 ml**
pinch	**cayenne**	**pinch**
	chopped parsley, to garnish	

GETTING READY

Make the pastry the day before, wrap and refrigerate overnight. Preheat the oven to 400°F/200°C and have ready a tray of 12 ungreased patty tins. Remove the pastry from the fridge, let it rest for 20 minutes, then roll it out on a floured board. Cut out 12 rounds of pastry and use them to line the patty tins. Chill the pastry-lined tins while you make the filling.

ASSEMBLY AND BAKING

1. Mix the remaining ingredients together in a saucepan, set over a medium heat and cook until the mixture thickens, stirring all the time. Set aside to cool for at least 10 minutes.
2. Spoon the filling into the pastry cases and bake for 20–25 minutes. Garnish with a little chopped parsley and serve warm. Makes 12.

Savoury Pinwheel Scones

Judging by its regular occurrence in community cookbooks, this was a popular type of savoury scone. The base is a plain scone dough, spread with a seasoned cheese and potato mixture, then rolled up and cut into slim spirals for baking. They are fairly substantial and so perhaps more suitable for morning tea than supper. This is based on a recipe from Wiki Paterson, who contributed it to the 1967 Karitane Public Hall Building Committee recipe book.

FOR THE DOUGH

1 cup	**flour**	**125 g**
1 tsp	**baking powder**	**1 tsp**
pinch	**salt**	**pinch**
	small piece of butter	**15 g**
½ cup	**milk**	**115 ml**

FOR THE FILLING

1 cup	**grated cheese**	**85 g**
1	**small onion**	**1**
½ cup	**chopped bacon**	**80 g**
½ cup	**mashed potato**	**½ cup**
1 tbsp	**chopped parsley**	**1 tbsp**
1	**egg**	**1**
½ tsp	**mustard***	**½ tsp**
	salt and pepper	

* or curry powder

GETTING READY

Prepare the mashed potato, which should be at room temperature, not hot. Preheat the oven to 425°F/215°C and line a baking tray with baking paper, or grease it lightly. Beat the egg lightly with a fork. Chop the onion, bacon and parsley finely, or whiz them in a food processor.

MIXING AND BAKING

1. Make the filling first by mixing everything together, using just enough of the egg to make a spreadable paste. Set aside.
2. Sift the dry ingredients into a bowl, rub in the butter and mix in the milk to form a soft dough. You may not need all the milk. Roll the dough out to a rectangle about 12 x 6 in/30 x 5 cm and 5 mm thick, spread with the filling and roll it up. Seal the edge by pressing the dough with your fingers and slice into pieces about ½ in/1 cm thick.
3. Place the scones on the baking tray and bake for about 10 minutes until nicely coloured. Wiki Paterson finishes her recipe with this comment: 'Rub over with buttered paper before removing from oven. This is a firm favourite.' (I brush them with a little melted butter.) Makes about 36.

Cooks and Books

COOKS
Some of the women whose recipes are included in this book:

Marian Benton, 1945

Joan Anderson, 1940

Tommie McArtney, with Peter and Paula, 1939

Paula Johnston, 1965

Myra Lawrie, 1948

Aphra Paine and Fiona Johnston, 2009

Mollie Newell, 1949

Nancy Yarndley, 1954

Marion Kitchingman, 1961

Marjorie Bond, 1942

Shirley Dunphy, 1966

Jeanette Nicholson, 1999

Liz Fumpston, 1978

Betty Shaw, 1935

Jocelyn Strewe, 1978

Kokila Patel, 2009

BOOKS
These are the recipe books which I used most often in my research for *A Second Helping.*

1920s
Tried Recipes, revised and published by the 'Ever Ready Committee' of The Victoria League, Auckland.

Manawatu Red Cookery Book, Tested and Tried Recipes, Palmerston North, 1926.

1930s
The Ideal Cookery Book, compiled by Ethel M. Cameron in aid of the Funds of the Plunket Society, Wellington Branch, 1933.

Aunt Daisy's Cookery Book of Approved Recipes, D. Basham, 1934.

Home Cookery Book, New Zealand Women's Institutes, 1939.

The N.Z. Daisy Chain Cookery Book Vol. No 2, by Aunt Daisy, containing over 800 Recipes and Hints, Mrs. D. Basham.

1940s
450 Favourite Recipes, Ladies Guild, St. Paul's Presbyterian Church, Pahiatua, 1946 – for church funds.

Aunt Daisy's New Cookery No. 6: Over 1400 New Recipes, second edition, Whitcombe & Tombs Ltd, 1947.

Aunt Daisy's Radio Cookery Book No. 4, Whitcombe & Tombs Ltd.

Dunedin City Gas Dept Cookery Book by Miss I. Finlay, twelfth edition.

The 'Diner's Digest', containing 800 selected choice recipes, published by the Auckland Travel Club Incorporated, 1941.

The Southland Patriotic Cookery Book In Aid of Patriotic Funds, compiled by Flora M. Crawford and Mary I. Lousley, Invercargill, 1940.

1950s
Dine with Elizabeth: a Round-the-year Book of Recipes, by Elizabeth Messenger, Parts one and two, Blundell Brothers Limited, Wellington, 1956 and 1957.

Khandallah Cookery Book, 422 tried and tested recipes, compiled by the Khandallah Presbyterian Church, A. H. & A. W. Reed, Wellington, 1950 – for a new church.

League of Mothers, 1926–1951, *Cookery Book and Household Hints*, Wellington, 1951.

St. Paul's Cookery Book, compiled by the Women's Fellowship of St. Paul's Presbyterian Church, Oamaru, 1956.

1960s
Cooking for Fun, The Tokoroa Free Kindergarten Association Inc., 1963 – for a new kindergarten.

Tastefully Yours, Waverley, Invercargill – for the Church and Church Centre Building Fund, 1963.

Our Recipe Book, compiled by the Karitane Public Hall Building Committee, Karitane, 1967 – for the Public Hall Building Fund.

The Menorah Cookbook, Jewish Women of New Zealand, 1963 – for the new Auckland Synagogue and Community Centre.

Margaret Bates, *Talking about Cakes, with an Irish and Scottish Accent*, Pergamon Press, Oxford, 1964.

1970s
Recipes: Old & New, compiled and published by Moana Rua Ladies and Brighton Life Saving Clubs – for the purchase of Surf Life Saving Buildings and Equipment to facilitate rescue.

Green and Gold Cookery Book, King's College, Adelaide, 31st edition. First printed 1923.

P.W.M.U. Cookery Book, Metric Edition, 1976 – for the work of the Presbyterian Women's Missionary Union of Victoria, Australia. First printed 1904.

1980s
Catholic Women's League Cookbook, Dunedin Diocese of the Catholic Women's League, 1981.

Recipe Book, St Columba's Presbyterian Church, Havelock North.

Michael Smith's Afternoon Tea: The Complete Book of Britain's Tea-Time Treats, Macmillan, London, 1986.

AND FOUR FAVOURITE COOKBOOKS:
Lois Daish, *Dinner at Home*, Bridget Williams Books, Wellington, 1993.

Lois Daish, *A Good Year*, Random House, Auckland, 2005.

Ray McVinnie, *The Modern Cook*, New Holland Press, Auckland, 2001.

Ray McVinnie, *Eat*, New Holland Press, Auckland, 2003.

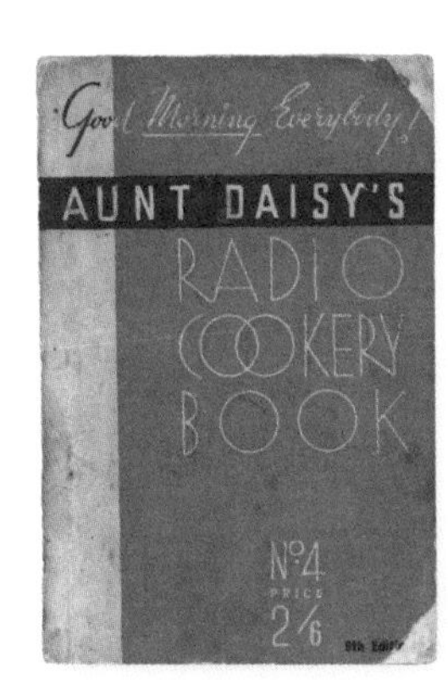

Aunt Daisy's Radio Cookery Book No. 4, Whitcombe & Tombs Ltd, Auckland circa 1940.

Acknowledgements

My first thanks goes to readers and bakers: to all those who bought copies of *Ladies, a Plate*, baked from it and told me that they enjoyed both the book and the baking. Their enthusiasm was the catalyst which encouraged me to embark on *A Second Helping* and I hope this new collection of recipes will prove equally enjoyable.

A number of friends gave or lent me books, recipes, information, and some of the embroidered cloths that appear in this book. Warmest thanks to Joan Anderson, Jill Bater, Marjorie Bond, Noeline Creighton, Bryony Dalefield, Bobbie Duthie, Bev Gotlieb Burgess, Rodney and Barbara Fumpston, Trish Gribben, Katherine Habershon, Christine Hellyar, Bridget Ikin, Fiona Johnston, Robyn Kelly, Setsuko Kennedy, Marion Kitchingman, Laura Kroetsch, Myra Lawrie, Dorothy and Ian McCarrison, Jenny Maidment, Chris Moor, Jenny Orange, Dean Parker, Kokila Patel, Colin Nicholson, Peter and Coral Shaw, Richard Smith, Jocelyn Strewe, Chris Szekely – and the wonderful Shirley Dunphy and her Tokoroa team.

Thanks also to Ray McVinnie and Lois Daish – my long-standing food heroes – for their friendship, wise encouragement, inspiring writing and brilliant cooking. As well as generously allowing me to include several of her recipes, Lois carefully read the whole manuscript and gave her customary perceptive comments. For their exemplary enthusiasm for the study of New Zealand's food history I thank Duncan Galletly, Helen Leach and David Veart.

I am grateful to the staff at Penguin New Zealand, especially Dorothy Vinicombe, Catherine O'Loughlin, Philippa Muller and Geoff Walker, and also to my editor Toni Mason, for their confidence and support.

At Inhouse Design, Arch MacDonnell, Sarah Gladwell and Dean Foster took my recipes and photographs and brilliantly created a book which I think is beautiful, witty and desirable – as well as useful. And with sterling assistance from Jane Hatfield, Shoba Pillai and Jason Mildren, the Inhouse baking critics nobly ate whatever I presented them with and gave me constant encouragement. (Thanks also to Gavin, Jaindra, Mia, Sadie and Geordie who assisted Inhouse with the chore of eating everything.)

To family and friends who assured me that my baking history explorations were indeed endlessly fascinating; to my niece Aphra for her invaluable practical help and especially to my husband, Malcolm Cheadle – my love and thanks, always.

Alexa Johnston
Auckland, April 2009

Index

PENGUIN BOOKS
Published by the Penguin Group
Penguin Group (NZ), 67 Apollo Drive, Rosedale, North Shore 0632, New Zealand (a division of Pearson New Zealand Ltd)
Penguin Group (USA) Inc., 375 Hudson Street, New York, New York 10014, USA
Penguin Group (Canada), 90 Eglinton Avenue East, Suite 700, Toronto, Ontario, M4P 2Y3, Canada (a division of Pearson Penguin Canada Inc.)
Penguin Books Ltd, 80 Strand, London, WC2R 0RL, England
Penguin Ireland, 25 St Stephen's Green, Dublin 2, Ireland (a division of Penguin Books Ltd)
Penguin Group (Australia), 250 Camberwell Road, Camberwell, Victoria 3124, Australia (a division of Pearson Australia Group Pty Ltd)
Penguin Books India Pvt Ltd, 11, Community Centre, Panchsheel Park, New Delhi – 110 017, India
Penguin Books (South Africa) (Pty) Ltd, 24 Sturdee Avenue, Rosebank, Johannesburg 2196, South Africa

Penguin Books Ltd, Registered Offices: 80 Strand, London, WC2R 0RL, England

First published by Penguin Group (NZ), 2009
3 5 7 9 10 8 6 4

Designed and typeset by inhousedesign.co.nz
Prepress by Image Centre, Ltd
Printed by Everbest Printing Co. Ltd, China

ISBN 978 014 320247 9

A catalogue record for this book is available from the National Library of New Zealand.

www.penguin.co.nz

COVER RECIPES
Lemon Bars page 38 and Easter Biscuits (without the currants) page 106

EMBROIDERY CREDITS
Cover and page 23 Linen afternoon tea cloth, designed in Glasgow and embroidered by Joan Anderson in 1940 when she was nineteen years old. Joan's skills and achievements extend far beyond embroidery and include being the first woman Moderator of the Presbyterian Church of Aotearoa New Zealand, 1979 – 1980. Page 12 Linen afternoon tea cloth embroidered in cross stitch by my grandmother, Tommie McArtney. Pages 60, 81, 83 White cotton cloth with cotton lace embroidery bought by Mrs Barbara Irvine in the Seychelles Islands and given to me by her daughter, Bobbie Duthie. Pages 66, 79 Square linen afternoon tea cloth given by Noeline Bruning to Bev Gotlieb Burgess, who gave it to me. Page 85 The cloth behind Sir Edmund Hillary's birthday cake is an apron made from yak wool, hand dyed and hand woven by Sherpa women in the Solu Khumbu region of Nepal. I bought it in Namche Bazar. Pages 25, 28, 51, 63, 105, 109 Embroidered cloths from Kalosca in Hungary. Page 143 Table runner with strawberries in knot stitch made in Kochi, Kerala, south west India and given to me by Bridget Ikin. Other cloths in this book are by embroiderers whose names, I regret, I do not know but whose beautiful work brings me pleasure every day.